A Storm of Horses

Other Books by Rob Ganson, and Long Lake Press

Float Like a Butterfly
Sing Like a Tree

and

Follow the Clear River Down

LONG LAKE PRESS

74705 Johannah rd.
Washburn Wi 54891
robostang@yahoo.com

A Storm of Horses

By Rob Ganson

Forward

To thank all of the fellow poets, friends, family members, and acquaintances who helped me find and refine my wee voice would take up a volume. You all know who you are, and what a vital place you have in my life, and my verse.

Another thank you goes out to the editors and publishers who took a chance on this, and other, emerging poets. Poetry is not a big seller in these fast-paced times, and publishing poetry in journals, magazines, books, is truly a labor of love.

Thanks to the teachers, police, and citizens of Wisconsin who marched together through the late winter and spring of 2011. As the priorities of thinking, caring people are usurped by the financial might of the 2%ers and their hired politicians, the need to speak truth to power is great.

Estuary, a Love Story was first published in Love Stories from the Bay, edited by Ros Nelson, and performed at Stage North in Washburn Wi

A New Freedom Song was first published by Verse Wisconsin in a series dedicated to the Wisconsin protests

Listen, and another selection were first Published by Kerouac's Dog Magazine.

Contents

The revolution will not…

I see my nation, my children, sold to the highest bidder,
see the hidden agenda of thin-blooded inheritors
sending Detroit bread to third world slave camps.
I see the purple mountain's majesty reduced to clear-cuts
and rivers of Hummers driving to a surrealistic inferno.
I shout NO! with my invisible voice, make a choice to battle
the beast with my little poems and placards, with a raspy
emphysema verse enhanced by a plastic bullhorn and a curse,
but shorn of power by citizens united through corporate dollars,
I holler into a wasteland of lemmings, parading over
their master's cliffs.

I see the watercress wave beneath the glass fluid
and I wonder how many miles of gravity separate the shards
of my brook from the corporate agripoison of the plains,
the deregulated sun, cooking it brown with yesterday's
topsoil, the toil of the family farmer replaced by
giant Deere, and Cargill's excess.

We put petrochemicals on the corn, corn in our tanks,
cow-fart mother's breath from fields of ureaformaldehide
and screams, douse our young men's dreams beneath
distant sands because our god is better than their god,
and odd fellows well met harvest the lucre watered by
the blood of every poor mother's mercenary son
because violence against our brothers pays better
than flipping burgers for burghers in SUVs that
need to eat quick and get back to working for the scraps
left them by forth-generation barons, stewing away
in hot tubs with a lap-full of silicone and fantasy.

I see the emperor of Wisconsin, feeding teachers to leeches,
cretins that preach capitalist excess to the carrion of a dying
middle class, see assholes in Cadillacs, flashing by all of us
in the passing lane, smirking at the fools who don't have the knack
for vampirism, who lack the soft pink hands of the kings
and the generals.

I watch the coalstacks bellow death so vidiots lose themselves
in front of entrancer screens full of rabid foxes preaching compliance
to the new order of serfs and slaves that see their way to
Mc Mansions through the haze of lotteries and the invective
of those who crave the mother's milk of unregulated donations,
who hold a bottle of Viagra in one hand, and their strings
in the other.

I wait for revolution, for evolution, any spark to ignite
the cause of right in the mind's eye of potentates,
to bask in the aura of peace that brotherhood generates
in the absence of war and greedy maps with cocked
and iron teeth.

I lay a wreath on the face of my brook, that it seek some
hidden nook of current in the Mississippi, that it heal
the river clear to the silent metaphor of New Orleans
and flood the very ocean with the simple honesty
of beauty.

I tend my garden as solemn duty, munch on gracious booty
bestowed on me and mine by the pregnant girth of earth
seasoned by a measure of vinegar, oil, and rapture.
I capture rain as if it is gold, behold magic as it takes hold
in the roots that connect me so surely that feet seem
twined to loam. There is no glory in the dirt, but only
connection to home, no lectern or pews, merely
sustenance that our dear mother grew.

I watch the evening news and feel like an Atlantian
on the cusp of the ocean, or a husk of a long dead flower,
feel like the darkest hour of man changes every sixty
minutes, like hope is the Dodo bird of our age, as
our only common denominators are pain and rage,
like a gerbil on the wheel in a burning cage.

we disengage from capitalist rule, celebrate lost
freedoms with vast tongues and slogans, shout our
obvious truths to oblivious leaders and decorate the ground
like Ohio teens the last time 'round, hound our masters
to relent? Should we engage the green-toothed machine,
and so enrage the kings that freedom cease to ring
in the voice of that cracked and aged bell?

Should we stand quietly backstage, assuage our guilt
with the gilded baubles that trickle down?

I wait for the age of Aquarius to dawn again, for
some son of peace to release us from the generals and bankers,
for truth and beauty, love and hope to rise like a Phoenix
from the ashes of a decayed civilization, but the revolution
will not…

Shadow Poet

What mayhem lurks behind this sharpest quill,
this instrument that hides my face with mask
of revolutionary chaos, spilled
in darkest ink to spell it's bloody task?

What ode, to quell the overlords of doom
may my dark imp provide to hide the meek
from the bankers and merchants, gods that loom
where truth dies as money-lenders speak?

Perhaps it takes a monster to spell one,
so I let my dervishes drive my pen
to expose darkest kings to light of sun
so wrath of simple men may rise again.

My monstrous yawp will penetrate the minds
of peaceful men, the hope for all mankind.

Sometimes it takes a monster
to open the blinds…

Glad Tidings from Jupiter

I would sing you glad tidings from Jupiter
but my feet are mired in mars,
sing you tales of congress with stars,
but the loam of home festoons
the midnight ears of barflies with
subliminal tunes in distant tongues.

If words could fly, I'd sling you high,
three flips over the roof of the sky,
like one 'o' them women flingers
on ice skates, or deliver you
a zero-gravity orgasm
on the far side of the moon,

but your troubadour can only manage
a love poem on a damp napkin
from a biker bar on the far side
of the SUVs and Christmas trees,
a stolen flower, the power
to disenchant the status quo
on the arm of a tattooed gnome
who calls an invisible castle home.

You live in a workaday world
but when my verbose flag unfurls
such misbegotten rhymes
that mothers shush me with pursed lips
and fingertips, like dismal editors,
mimes from the temperate climes
who clamor for Dick and Jane,
or a Billy Collins poem
no one needs to explain,
Billy's little jokes seem quite arcane.

Darlin' I'll sing you the colors you lack,
take you back to paisley days
beyond the facts to sheer conjecture,
forward to the rivers of tomorrow,
just put on your pink helmet
and climb on back.

The Three Sheets Concerto

I

She emerged from the river
with a shiver, a wraith
at the gates of gravity.

II

I followed the clear waters
to a woman who filled
the hollows of me with sonnets,
with birdsong and lullabies,
with stealthy elfin phonics,
with a longing for music words
seldom heard but for
the gracious ears of dawn.

III

She would be the one, the sun
that would spark my very days
and mark my nights with glee,
and years of twisted sheets
would bear witness to fleeting
paintings, written on the leaves
that sing of the divine, that mark
my time with stanzas of mirth,
with rhyming lines of birth, vistas
of rivers, caressing the very face
of the earth that spawned my muse.

Emphysema

Oh, that sharp intake, the surprise
of a few more lines, another soliloquy,
or a discourse with the sublime.

On what leaves will these extras,
these unexpected breaths
array themselves
as flames from a broken bellows?

Oh shame, that gift words
murmur in mirrors, as if the day
speaks only its name.

Stanza

Poetry is a dance of words
in the eyes of a lover,
a picture spelled in song,
or a moan in fourteen lines
from the sharpest quill
to whisper secrets
to a reader's
soul.

The North Star Concerto

I

She, alpha, wild - sings
and the night rings wild
Sojourners spark and turn
as their natures wake
to take life from her

II

Curs, poseurs in the distance
remark in pale imitation
bark in abeyance of wings
sing as if they too run
the meat circle

III

Coyotes join in bright notes
in silver coats, warm against night
and the fright ignites
in lesser finery of rabbit
and a man runs asleep

Peeing on Buddha

It happens every damn time I drink tequila.
There he sits in his circle of yellow
brittle grass, his little kingdom,
surrounded by flowers, butterflies,
his friend, the toad.

But daddy drank a buttload 'a' cactus juice,
and half-a-monster has been loosed
on the gentle kingdom
of hummingbirds and hope.
There may even be dope involved.

The music is blaring, the moon glaring
from her aura of lights,
ladylove is being wooed, seemingly
by all three stooges,
and there I am, teetering
on the front of the deck,

(OOPS!)

peeing on Buddha.

Acorn

She tucked herself with a thump
against loam, blanketed the future
with Halloween swaddling.

Rainsnowcoldrainwarmhot, and
her fine young Jesus reached
for the vulture's distant phrases,
for psalms from a balmy oracle.

When the carapace cracked,
the sapling, bound by anthems
and misbegotten pride, died on
sand bereft of blanket or glory,

but what of the boy; a soldier,
a metaphor, or a fine young
cannibal with an axe?

What of the confused poem,
dropping on this leaf
with a thump?

After the Fall

Unfiltered orb, and green leaves fall.
Prairies crisp, so gold, so seared,
so tall, golden by July from greed,
from unthinking loins bright seed.

Ponds recede as dinosaurs light dusk
with neon and the stench of musk.
Oh man, bipedal virus, assassin
of the last dry-footed iris, wan husk,

what hope remains for our verdant womb?
What measure to avert advent of tomb?
Headlong, we rushed to seal our fate,
with all the machines that we create.

Unfiltered orb, and the wasteland bakes
while ice caps melt, the ring of fire shakes.
The songbirds have gone, and the bees.
The graves are marked by skeletal trees.

Ghost Walk

 I am taken aback at yesterdays found
lacking in substance. Ephemeral, I
reach for wisps of whatithinkiwas
to chew on past glory, or surrealist
bits of gory wishihads…

but, nothing is there waiting
like tomorrow's glad canvas
or the best idea I'll never have.

I try to catch moments, like
lightningbugs to place inajar,
but now is too far to reach
for arms too short to read.

Starlit

Gilded by the ponderous weight of stars
sweat-varnished by july she
oh she
        radiant she

rode through the night like
cupid's cavalry

(oh firefly neon
oh swoon

what finer potion wafts
on midnight's breath

than whispered sighs
where friction meets
fusion

and the moon wears
                        breasts)

Notes on Dancing with a Poet

When he makes my hips dance
to the softest music of words
that awaken hidden rhythms,
poetry is the author
of his touch –

and phrases that anoint my flesh
with the full flush of love
meld him with Pablo's ghost
on the gentle landscape
of a muse.

Modern Primitive

I know a guy that lives like me,
pursuant to nature's laws,
with wooden arms,
and steel tipped claws.

I know a place where watercress
dwells amid cold and tiny
currents, rivulets of wonder
and clarity.

I know a poet that cooks his stew
with adjectives and garlic, with
metaphors that renew the spirit
of lilting phrase.

I know a dog that loves like a poet,
that runs as a storm, and points
the way an artist paints scenes
of grace.

I know a river that speaks in tongues,
fables of endless circles, cycles
of round ripples in an unnatural
world of squares and sooty lungs.

I know how the rain tastes
on the last lap
of a long race.

Red Ink

Here is my blood, my blue entrails,
strewn across a blank field
in stormy metaphor.

Here is my fondest night, my eclipse,
my doom and rapture, hidden
in verbose riddles.

Here is my greatest fear, my dismal
reckoning of greed's dark seeds,
my universal confession.

Here is my immortality, festooning
future eyes with grand gibberish,
and a lax accounting

for punctuating

bombs bursting in air

with rivers of blood
from children.

I Called her Dot

Her skin was speckled like catfish flanks
and soft as passion's sigh
Nigh onto manhood, I counted them
like sacred stars in some newfound
constellation
that left me breathless
like an astronaut
reading his way to heaven
by braille

14

Anonymous

Dear Joan,

I miss you when the cumulous lubricates
like you would have that day under the
boardwalk if you had felt me there.

Remember that first time I didn't kiss you
beneath the arc of mars, the tug of tide?

The first time my lips, my tongue, found
those secret rhythms hidden where your hips
meet your own song, I sung along like some
evangelical supplicant, or a gaudy squeezebox,

but you weren't, I wasn't, and the moment
was as lost as our anniversary, the Dodo
of all the nows that never occurred, and
I never verbed your sweetest noun.

I wasn't quick yet with sap or witty
foreplay when Billy punctuated your
forehead with your last period, but I
swooned, just the same, because we
never had our threesome with Zelda,

but you must know, my dear,
it would have been
spectacular…

Anonymous

Not a Product

Our leaders have been reduced to products,
bottom feeders that practice random acts
of malignant capitalism, leaders that bend
the facts into pretzel-logical tornadoes
of innuendo to further the interests of the
big green dynamo, the ho that flows
with the rhetoric of the damned to advance
the plans of that motherfuckin' two percent.

You are not black, white, yellow, or red,
but a member of a demographic group,
a human soup that the corporate giants slurp
with the gusto of vampires at a blood drive,
and we, the wordslingers, need to keep the truth alive.
We need to ride in to fuckin' Dodge and hurl
the truth like a verbose spear, shout it
into every open mic until every fleeced sheep
hears it, until every member of the doomed middle class
hears through the lies from the assholes at Fox
and stops voting against themselves, against
their children.

We need to take America back from the soft pink
Viagra popping leeches that sucked all the jobs
into the recesses of the third world so Barbie
could wear a couple extra diamonds to celebrate
the excess of the useless inheritors they married.
We need to take America back from a black man that
made blue promises, spilled a flood of red blood
from brown men, and rules for the mighty green.
He sends the poor to fight for oil, while his hands
stay clean.

We got to speak up for the single mother, for
the unemployed; got to speak up for one-another
before the only voice left is the dollar, got to holler
with poetry, with raps and rhymes, 'cause now is the time
to throw our words into that green machine
before all we got left is masters 'n' slaves,
before the American dream is buried in a golden grave.

The best minds of my generation sold out,
sold out to become corporate whores for more money,
more power, a bigger slice of a less than humble pie.
We lie and cheat, we deregulate and greet each new day
with a quest for more, more, more, while the pink slug
at the company store buys a new set of tits for his whore.
The presidents give the wealthy free rein while the
lowly residents feel the pain of lost jobs, lost benefits,
and those two percenters gain every time the rest of us lose,
lose the right to choose, the right to collectively bargain,
lose the right to fair compensation, lose the right to
representation, while the "SUPREME" court gives all the power
to the bazzilionaire of the hour, and exchanges liberty
for a system of for the few, and by the few.

I AM NOT A PRODUCT
but a wordslinger extraordinaire, a poet that's grown a pair,
a poor and simple man that dares to speak, hell, to shout
truth in the face of power, and if you shout with me, if you
raise your voices in this night of our discontent, if you stand tall
and demand that the vampires relent, and share the pie,
and fight for your rights, and your neighbors rights,
if you demand, DEMAND your propers, we just might light a spark;
we might ignite a fire that burns hot and bright enough
to light the way to freedom once again,

we might…

won't you help?

Lay Me Down

Lay me down on the cool side of the pillow
Spread me out 'cross the garden's face
Lay me down when my path has ended
and I've found the way to grace

Don't respond with tears or misery
when you spread me on the ground
'cause the garden feels my energy
as the circle comes around

There's endless air in Xanadu
to fill much longer lines
with everlasting poetry
in books that need no spines

Lay me down in the loving part of your mind
where rivers run and children play
lay me down on a shelf of poets
but read me when skies turn gray

I'll never really die, my dear
but merely shed this mortal host
to make words dance aloft
as whispered by a ghost

Spread my nutrients on the ground
Let flowers spell my name
but shed no tear for a poet
who left at the top of his game

Lay me down where there ain't no generals
no lawyers or other such thieves
Lay me down to close the circle
like autumn's cloak of leaves

Notes on Growing Small

when the sidewalk is split by the flower
or the temple by the tree
we are connected by these…
in my transient skin…i remember
how soon i will feed my garden

it is not moot to ponder
whether pity is a selfish act
when I behead another
cabbage…

and my roots begin
to show

Storming the Gates of Heaven

What adjective must I invoke
to provoke a swoon in ladylove
that I may verb that lovely noun?

I would but map the way to grace
by following secret rhythms
of such fond geography

that the path of moon mimic
her dancing hips.

A Wordslinger's Creed

I ain't no Billy Collins or even uncle Walt; more like a placard waving revolutionary,
trying to halt the wars.

I ain't no dead-ass poet that taped up the windows and doors to put an exclamation point
on a pointless death, but a breathless old motherfucker that still stutters out long lines to define another route for a bunch of lemmings and fools, tools of the neo-corporate, jewel bedecked,
war-mongering collective of rich old white men that suck the very blood from the middle class, the loud, drawn-out last gasp of the post-beat subculture of old dead Allen, devoid of the brainwashed Dick and Jane shit that Billy spews, the truth behind the lies on the evening news.

I'm the voice of the worker that struggles in the talons of a corrupted eagle, the voice of an oily albatross, hundreds of years old, a pro-choice, peacenick that believes the next president should be a grandmother, another sort of poet altogether, a resident of the nation of the open mind, stammering, yammering the very truth in a nation of liars and thieves, a loud-mouthed agitator that aggravates the kings behind the gates of steel, the squeak in the wheels of justice. I'm one of the leaves from Walt's book, a peek into the nook of the collective consciousness of those who know better than to follow the blind, the kind of guy the blue-haired mink wearing queens of commerce cross the street to avoid, the voice of the void between atoms, leaning so far left that the kings are exposed as the foes of freedom, the frightening poem in a magazine.

I'm a nail in the wheel of "progress," a progressive with a half-empty bottle of tequila,
throwing darts at the tea party, winning hearts and minds with verbose arrows of light
to push back the night, to shine a bright beacon on the path of peace in a world gone mad, the mad hatter at the tea party of the damned, a burr under the saddle of the fucktard in the ten-gallon hat, airing out my belfry in the lexicon of bats.

"Yo, Deejay, crank up the volume to a hundred and three, 'cause the truth will set you free!" The truth about Cheney and Bush, the truth about torture, the truth about tax cuts for the rich, and the bitch wearing Newt's diamonds, the truth about Afghanistan, Iraq, Pakistan, and all the other plans of destruction in the name of a long dead peacenick, the truth about the bringer of change that fails to re-arrange anything except his own priorities now that he is mighty, that forgets the meek that gave him his crown, the guy that voted for the clown that fooled us all, the truth about the subsidies for bankers while the rank and file dines on Ramen Noodles and lost dreams, the sound of the screams from Palestine, the truth about the schemes to make the rich richer and the poor invisible, the truth about global warming and the loss of the family farm, the truth about all the folks harmed in the names of mirror gods and corporate government. the hungry mouth that hovers over the open mic, the truth about my failure to leave my progeny a viable world, the truth about expansionism, and the bloody flag unfurled over every war over oily sand, the truth about an ineffectual man who takes a stand for the homeless in a land of plenty.

No, I'm no Billy Collins, but only a wordslinger that hopes to linger long enough
to point a finger at that hungry vampire behind the curtain, before we join the dinosaur
in the mire of another failed species.

The Man in the Mirror

It must have been a Monday
when the old man appeared in my mirror.
His scars looked like my poems,
and he seemed to seek absolution
for his part in some dismal drama.

I saw him again in clear waters,
washed, cleansed of myriad sins.
I fed the homeless man, met anger with glee,
and started trying to kill war with poetry.

Perhaps I can spell redemption in a mirror.

Notes on the Nature of Things

But, my things do not own me
or extravagance define my stature,
and home is not my own hearth
but the forest that holds my heart.

I am god like the bees, the trees,
the toad, full of warts, that holds
court over his dank niche as a softer
Buddha, god, like a hummingbird.

I am simpler than my nod to commerce,
simpler than the sum of my station,
measured by green leaves or inflation,
simple as the brook that seeks the river
and finally the sea, simple as a breast.

If a far flung pebble chased ripples
to some bright infinity, my flute would
seek its song with cedar intonation
that mimics geometric fractals, divulged
in the feathers of a loon's finery, and so
seek flight beyond the birth of rain
to some clear nation of the soul.

Sparks fly from the eye of the raven in
his search for tiny deaths, that wholesome
compost of wrappers, devoid of absent hosts,
ghosts in the cosmic machine of earth.

I am not static, not of any moment
or disciple of some divined image,
not of a proud mirror of glass, but real,
actual, in the liquid mirror of a pond
where ripples spread like guidelines
to a circle that joins us all.

Notes on Pablo's Physics

Does love lie at the base of a cliff
from which one must gladly leap,
or virus-like seep into we, stealthy
as if to infect us with metaphysical
tidings of something more,
(some geometric merging of fractals)
and so sound a song for two
that is sung, writhing in breaths
of copper and warm oceans
to resuscitate dreams of magic?

Love exists in the space between
our atoms, where flowers feed on shit,
and joy is measured by tiny deaths,
falling like rain, and we shudder
beneath the lovely weight of blooms
born of untouchable moments.

Finding Myself in a Confession

I find myself basking on the shore of Marc Creamore's "Bohemian
Highway" taken aback at the things my mouth tells my fingers to say,
wringing arthritic mental hands at the truing of them. I measure the task
of peace as if, by lunchtime, the monster's thirst be quenched by a rain
of metaphorical butterflies, its hunger sated by the shock and awe of
barbequed children, of split atoms, burned dinosaurs, ranks of sun-eyed
children at attention, pledging allegiance to angry factions and
expansionist wars. I find myself "Biking the Wings of Giant Birds"
with Danny Beatty, looking down at cogs, wheels, gears, asphalt,
growing like ectoplasm, mayhem; looking down at an ant-poet, trying

to kill war with a placard, with a rhyme, and a fantasy of something holy, looking down at a jester in a graveyard of dreams, but the Swan rises like an organic airliner, bound for Nirvana, and the farms spread out like emerald blankets, vegetative afghans, knitted by grandmothers, and given to the callused, sun-dried hands of the few who feed all. I find myself wishing Jim Dunlap could edit my lungs like he edits my sonnets, adjective them with expansive, elastic, healthy, viable, or edit me into my own Loon Lake, and call me not Icarus. I see my callused fingertips where Buddha looks after the kingdom of the toad, see them brush that stone belly, not so much like a genuflection, as a genuine reflection of hope that a jolly belly holds hope, even when it graces a small stone man in a garden where toads and poems grow. I see myself grow translucent in the mirror, and know that guy is on his third pair of ever-strengthening reading-glasses, but only because his arms are short, and only for poetry readings, but he is still way too cool for a beret, or even a clean shirt, too cool for Birkenstocks with socks, too cool to fuel the Republican fund-razor with pseudo-patriotic bullshit and glamor, too cool to fool with nonsense that colors colonialism in the red, white, and blue lies about freedom, too cool to kill for ol' uncle Sam in distant lands. I see myself on salty shores, waxing circular with Zayra and Marc, marking time in love and kindness offered, marking pebbles with rakes of song and wonder, wondering if the Yin and Yang of pleasures pressured to wait and hurry in fact affect tides, or if tea may flavor a flute with peaceful anthems. I see myself on red cliffs overlooking the mother of waters, pulled North and South with waters that seek differing seas, pulled to heaven and the soil on the cusp of some great voyage. I see myself weeping for my fellows, strewn along a path from revolution and enlightenment to resignation and acceptance. We have forsaken the yellow brick road for the asphalt jungles, forsaken the jungles and gardens for a green paper trail to hell, forsaken our children for the spoils of oil and maps that grow like cancer, and have cannibalized our offspring for lazy-boys and ever larger entrancer screens, decorated with endless products. I find myself quiet in the faces of bigots and thieves that pay me to recreate them on fields of green, that pay me to bow and scrape like a pale negro with invisible chains, weeping at necessary compromises in the name of armies of children I urge not to prostitute themselves as we have done, and all the while singing my beautiful lies, as if by painting myself holy, I erase my sins against my mother's verdant breast, erase the best of me with a hardening heart that stutters like an often broken engine, stutters those frigid words, "I Thought I could, I thought I could, I thought..." I can attest to all these sins and more, attest to my own failure in the greatest test of all, admit that my quest to kill the wars has failed, and so accept whatever island a soiled soul may beach itself on, come graduation day. I find myself blinking at the growling sun, chanting sonnets as if to decorate the wind with the screams of all the napalmed innocents, chanting my sad dramas of "doasisaynotasido," reciting the mad beat dogma of the lost one who is afflicted with every nuance of personal responsibility for the grievous acts of my fellows, scratching away at the future pilgrim's minds with a cheap pen in yellowed fingers. Oh, what great pharmacist, what vast alchemist can cure such woe? I stubbed my toe on reality, and my soul turns purple as the crowning nail. What respite has a woebegone wordslinger to partake of to find the sun in a soot-filled world? I climb the verbal libraries of Patterson to find a mantra of possibility, some verbose recipe to sprinkle hope on this thin and melancholy soup, but the evening news is festooned with corpses and tidings of pride in bombs bursting in air, tidings of madmen with troves of ammunition and porn. I see myself shorn, torn, adrift, bereft of the gods men conjure to forgive themselves lives like mine, godless on an accelerating circle that seems prepared to fling me off. I sing the bloodied pacifist, the extinct family farm, the unsullied choir of children in the throes of joy, absent the need for riches or acclaim, the storm of the last wild horses, blowing across the very last plain, the hummingbird, the toad, so free of ego in his moist and happy squalor. I holler epithets at the unquestioning hero with the big fucking gun, shout NO at the puppet master with marionettes in white houses and television sets, scream long lines from a short-lined bellows, bellow peace songs to the dogs of war. I see myself hiding in my garden, hiding in a good woman's arms, hiding beneath the dust of unread libraries, hiding in the oil-slick feathers of Sam's albatross, hiding in the darkest halls of shame, hiding behind every name for failure, every excuse for dead dreams and altruistic endeavor, forsaken in the name of commerce, forsaken to escape the blame for the tanks that roll on without a poet's body to paint their treads red, forsaken by my own device. I find myself in the bank, scribbled in small denominations, in the search for higher meaning, in the leaning tower of greed, in the need to feed the monster my own weak hunger, in the journals of every poet that failed to write our flawed species a way to peace, in the release of my seed into the womanly receptacle that is too holy to harbor my dis-ease, and, all the while, stumble across a list of misdeeds, of good deeds undone. Oh grief, oh thief of hearts, that seeks to cloud the verge of some verdant garden, release me from such ponderous cause that failure is certain before, on the verge of that distant shore, I find myself

guilty.

Notes on Thin Soup

Tenuous, our hold on such as gods,
our grasp of this thin ledge, called
                    hope

and, paper-thin, these odes of love
that smolder on such hungry lips,
                    dreaming

that someday, he/she will love like
poets do, like the very earth loves
                    rain.

Our hearts beat behind gauzy veils
that filter pain like noxious grains
                    of reality.

Hidden behind my bygone caul, I
craft my daft missives, sonnets for
            whoipretendsheis.

While the coyotes tempt my flute, I
sip at a warm bowl of thinnest soup,

                    unrequited.

A Bench for Two

When the sand runs thin in the hour glass,
and reality seems like a dark cloud,
one may give in to alack and alas.
I offer a space where no pain is allowed.

A glade, green with ferns, lit by filtered sun,
on the soft verge of a clear-running stream,
a simple bench for a man and his son,
a special healing place, crafted of dreams.

You'll meet a woman there, gentle and kind,
who will understand your need of this place.
In this fair land, your very dreams align
with some sacred spirit, some kind of grace.

In this special place, each dawn is a gift,
each labored breath, each reluctant heartbeat,
another smile, another flower sniffed.
This dream I offer is yours to complete.

When you throw a pebble into a pond,
this is where perfect circles go to play.
This place is a peek at the great beyond,
a place beyond pain to greet each day.

If you meet a poet, fighting for breath,
don't worry; that's just me, denying death.

Notes from a Greyhound Bus

Rocking,
she kept rocking an invisible baby
to the time of the long dog's gait,
murmuring something, a name perhaps,
or some missing
                    incantation.

There seemed to be a tall shadow
behind her, a weight that pressed her
into this rhythmic service, a trailer park
and dead cars
                in her eyes.

The shadow wasn't me, I know it, but

the yellow dashes Morsed stories
I didn't want to hear, that I couldn't
                              survive.

I think it was near Memphis
or perhaps Omaha, somewhere
south of Purgatory, when I was broken,
well and finally broken by the sound
of a

        lullaby.

Sweet Child of Mine

Sweet child of mine, each morning is a gift
and each new dawn, another battle won.
Each flower's song that you inhale adrift
on gentle winds is like a rising sun.

Each day with you is like a blooming bud
that paints our world the very shade of hope
and every smile you give, another flood
of happiness that gives us strength to cope.

Your lot in life is not an easy one
but your strong little spirit shines so bright
that even though your life has just begun
everyone who meets you bathes in it's light.

Your lot in life is not an easy one
but love will keep you strong, my sweet wee son.

American, me

I will not write of bloody-handed heroes
Or varnish-haired kings
Not extol empires of things
Or over-burdened sweat-pants, meandering
Down the yellow brick aisles
At Wal Mart
But of shine-faced mothers, killing
War with placards and songs, the
Leather-skinned farmer
Feeding the planet,

the rivers at play

To Live in Verse

I see her wearing birds and flowers
as if the years and hours since
were not, and she is yet

When the bumblebirds sip
at plastic diners
    she is sweet
and I weep at pictures
of the queen of Xanadu

I see her in clear running streams
and it seems as if gooseflesh
is available for today's

kiss

I read her in bittersweet poems
dancing, always dancing
and I the swaying thistle with the
   invisible partner

     held close

She is so white now
the egret hibuscus

I see her dancing when the fiddle sings
and forever seems

lovely

What's the Matter?

Is it if my eyes can drink it in
or hands weigh its girth?
If I dream of coathooks
in fresh-scented pine
will they support
the frayed Carhartts?

If I verb a noun
will it dance across the page
like a rubber ball
or practice the stasis atoms
forget?

Is she, that glad hands explore
or merely some figment
of synapse married protons?

When germination's green hand
reaches for the sun
the soil becomes actual
once I see it, once I freeze time
but only if you see it too.

Only the moment matters.

When we fight no more...forever

I want to be a turtle
And retreat from wars
Into my self-bunker

I want Wile E. Coyote
Forgotten, alone
In his puff of dust

To Sing with Frogs

is this the last frog's song
that stirs such lethargic limbs
to dance away the blue

heart of winter
that so envelopes the soul
that an autumnal lover sings
of beginnings

does that willow-haired sky weep
of endings or stroke the thighs
of ladylove with the first
true rhythms

the garden speaks of birth and decay
as a poet wonders how personally
he will feed it

will the pine verb itself away
for the eyes that drank it
like a potion, like a ladder
to the clouds

a heart bursts like daffodil bulbs
at the songs of mating
the glad spiral of woodcock
the distant drum of grouse
the subliminal sheen
of fresh layed eggs

the dew did not freeze today
or the new sonnet fail
to free her secret smile

perhaps, I'll stay awhile
to sing with the frogs

My Inner Boy

The world is trying to kill my little boy
Kill him with hungry vaults and myriad
Oil wars with adjectives like patriotic
And ambitious nouns like ambition
And recompense nouns like god and
General nouns like bomb and profit
And the other prophet verbs like worship
Obey procreate infiltrate abrogate initiate
Action words like subjugate and rape
But my little boy lives to push their shame away
To dance in poverty naked in the garden
He thinks the human breast is more holy
Than a church full of mirrors and demands
More holy than myths or filthy dollars
More holy than the priest that bends
The boy over the altar of some angry
God he painted on the back of innocents
More holy than any crusade or tithe
More holy than a bank full of doubloons
More holy than a bloody-handed soldier
Who reduces other mother's children
To twitching leaking disjointed limbs
And returns home to fireworks and acclaim
More holy than piles of reeking dollars
In the soft pink hands of bloated leeches
He thinks the lullaby more holy than the hymn
Or the anthem and peace more holy than victory
Oh the man in me succumbs to bills and blisters
To laws against joy to well-armed wolves at the diner
To flickering images that tell him to buy the finer things
To the tax man with diamond rings and M-16s
To the giant that reduces him to notations on the time clock
To the presidents and kings to the false construct of dollars
But he struggles against his thorny collar for his boy
The boy that remembers the scent of bliss
The boy that knows that really knows
That no amount of lucre is worth the value
Of a freely given kiss that knows the green in banks
Is not sacred like the greens from the garden

That knows that the apple is more holy than judgement
You can find my little boy traipsing naked
In the forest or weeding a garden by hand
Find him walking the land with gentle feet
Find him dancing for no apparent reason
Find him mumbling incantations from Rockland
And Xanadu from the Tao and Walden pond
Find him intoning invitations to ladylove
Invitations to join him on the path to joy
but there is one place you will never find my boy
never find the man one land we will never explore
one landscape that we both abhor

We will never partake of war

The Night of the Frogs

The season of the frogs began last night
with such a chorus of spring and rebirth
that our loins quickened to songs of delight
as if such writhing forms covered the earth.
Love songs echo from the forest, the creek
from the very sky, as worlds come to life.
The winter's grasp, so strenuous and bleak
relents, as every husband seeks a wife.
The crocus and daffodil pierce the veil
of ice that so encapsulates the land
as diverse lovers read their bliss by Braille.
Pistils grow to meet life's sweetest demand.
Winter dies in a burst of frenzied song
and I, my friends, can't help but sing along.

Watching Indigo

I watched Indigo Moor read
For seven people in a library
In a library where empty chairs sat
Like vultures at the last supper

I watched academic scythes
Lopping off the heads
Of adjectives and art

He showed me Robert Johnson
Choking on poison, 'cause
He forgot to pick a homely gal
Choking on poison, like
A perfessor, choking
On word-music, choking
On beauty
And my mind's eye saw
Billy Collins on publican radio
Killing poetry with Dick and Jane

I watched Indigo Moor read
For seven people in a library
And I heard a thousand
Thousand books weeping
In solitude

I saw a pushcart running over
Dick and Jane
I saw squadrons of hummingbirds
Darting bland poets
With iridescent hues
And news of bright phrases
Dancing in the air like

Hope

I watched Indigo Moor read
For seven people in a library
During national poetry month
And for a moment
The irony   faded

2011

The wolves have gathered in Washington's aisles
to feast on herds of blind and silent sheep.
Hidden in the lies of those bloody smiles
innocent bones gleam, and peasants sleep.
The cupboard is bare and the mortgage, due
but the vultures still thirst for working men.
They steal from the many, give to the few
feast on our children, and send them again
to kill in the desert, to kill for oil
as if the whole world is theirs to pillage
and as the serpent's seven lengths uncoil
rubble and smoke mark another village.
Seeing another soldier's floral wreath
I wonder if it's time the sheep grew teeth.

The Dance of Adolescent Adjectives

Something comes in the night,
Comes with hunger for moist secrets
Comes with hidden violence, whispering
Sweet refrains, "You know I love you, baby."
But a steel piston shrieks for oil
And sweet calamities blur inner vision
With folds of vulnerable muse
With armor of white cotton
And an opening bud that calls me god
Again and again   but I see it in some mirror
Like a skyscraper full of windows
Wearing my face
And when I wake I know, nothing
Will ever be the same

After

But, what of the Yin when my bellows fail?
When two make one beneath the smile of sun
and read the sum of bliss by dint of braille
what grace remains for that surviving one?

When loving arms that held me oh so close
embrace the empty night, what joy awaits?
I would not have her bound to ancient ghosts
or caught by stasis our lost love creates.

Her wisdom so guided strong hands and back
that a gentle father grew from such rough stock
and every fine impulse her husband lacked
sprung from some forgotten well she unlocked.

And when I've gone to walk some unknown land
I hope some worthy lover takes her hand.

Now

The moment was not, it seems, born to hold
as pregnant now never fully gestates.
Static protagonists try to unfold
tomorrow as the very it abates.

I am, I know, the past's own abductee
that struggles to pry now and then apart
but present hides, and I, an amputee
must try to find my way bereft of chart.

A particle of time, fleeting, wary
is sought headlong, an effort to distill
the bliss of today, to meet and parry
tomorrow's thrust with momentary thrill.

This very instant, fleeting and arcane
lives despite proofs of yesterday's remains.

Between

I live in between
Monday and death
like a photo

lying
in an album

that pleads the fifth
between pages

proclaiming the existence
of now.

Only a Kiss

Oh kiss that so proclaims our tender lust
that lovers speak in tongues
and breath is whispered
to mingle in trust.

Oh meeting lips that sip at bliss
as if we meet between us
in such a soft regard
that souls may merge

like this.

Spring Creek

oh, the things found
            bythestream

gleam, gleem those effervescent
birdsongs in birthing sun

  (as if the answer is sap)

and drinkdrinkdrink
the syrup of my love's fire
from lips such breasticular

dancing and jugglingjiggles
    from lip's fount
            from mounting

mountains with whiskered
            cheek

(oh, nipplequickening ministrations)

even daffodils
yapyapyap, even yawp

    the sum of spring's bright

baubles

and that the yellow thaw impose
the martial law
            on her repose

(oh, sun's first tentative fingers)

dewlubricated mournings
of poorlostdeath

frosted peaches relent

        exposed, warm

as the sappan boils
(her skin boils perspiration's birth)

the whippoorwill, ne'er-do-well
sprung from blue
wellofsouls

(oh, great hot girth of thislust)

becoming becoming becoming
(to crickmusic and blatant days)

belay those cold insinuations

to play with ladylove
    draped in trust and light

(beside a gentle stream)

Another Clichéd Spring Love Poem

I love you the way
my deaf dog loves
my breath

the way the sun
loves glass
and skin

and in that tender grasp
the sum of us
blooms.

Now and Zen

The pen leaves a poem on the page
a poor lost now, splayed across the parchment
like a corpse, viewed at a wake.
Whitman froze time, and Blake
and now did not forsake Coleridge
but painted his winter eyes with lace.
A place, painted with the brush of grace
is but a landscape
colored by textures and nouns
but, oh, a kiss, a blow, a primal scream
frozen in a poet's words
may gleam like a leprechaun's gold
or the very coin of whimsy
rising in the loins of yesterday's love
may freeze forever the meeting of lips
first brush of loving fingertips
the approach of snowflake to pine
the flash of synapse in an over-revving mind
and so, bestow that fleeting now
to the eyes of tomorrow's static reader
and so extol the virtue of such fleeting reality
that that reader draw one deep breath
knowingly, and expose a frozen thought.
Oh, yin, oh, yang, oh trusted river of time
how unfaltering, the sun's climb of sky
or winter's frigid grasp
how sure the last gasping stanza
that tries to pry today from tomorrow's claws
but, if your eyes should find these rhymes
these meek missives
frozen in time
stuck between winter and spring,
each line, a moment of ethos or joy
a pregnant particle of present
a coy smile at immortality

perhaps a moment may be mined
to stand the test of time
and so refute tomorrow
in dancing eyes that know
the next day never arrives.
Circumspect lives with eyes for tomorrow
effect the future with bills, maps
and momentless men
milking life for paper recompense
and the evidence lies in too much stuff
and wars to gather more.

Remember, now is all we ever have.

For now, the snowflakes stop
reaching for the crocus
soldiers freeze before report
while an old man writes an odd photo
of a stone Buddha, resting
in the American snow
on a Monday, with nowhen else
to go.

Dancing Barefoot

Sun-clothed, laughing, we spun 'round the maypole
like pinkfrogdervishes playing with life
and later, when protuberances gathered sap
we reached for the moon with glad limbs.
Naked feet reached for soil, and music kept
them shuffling, gliding, while the moon
crooned like simple drums, playing tides
into rivers while wooden flutes warbled.
It is in our feet to dance like this
for feet to touch the earth with glad pats
and hips to sing the moon's circle.

Shame will not find us dancing
or clothe us in armor against joy
and awash in sun's warm glow
we dance to holy rhythms
barefoot, from head to toe.

Everyman

I got laid in a cheap motel -
the one with the empty pool
and the flickering neon no sign
halfway between nowhere
and somewhere

                    *

Men and women can never be friends
without the cloud of loins hanging
over them like an empty
cartoon dialog bubble

Moonshadow

We were like two nations of elves
who melded maps into moist silk nights
and blamed the whole thing on the dancing.

The ahhs, the giggles and guffaws of our
twisting tongue's chicanery mingled
with streamsong to decorate decades
with lovestains on dawn's bright sheet.

Not shrill, a harpy crooning duty
but lilting strains of love like flowers
wafting from a garden, painted
on the breeze by she

but she, you see, must do without me

and if need arise, can she dance
as if the sun is whole and sky alight
over a kingdom with one polished stone?

By the moon's lingering tingle
on yin's sweet geography will she spark
as if one star remains of our sky
and each well kissed waypoint remember
the fading portrait of elven touch.

She will paint the soil with dancing tracks -
the night with such delight that shadows
from the moonlight tell old stories
of a crone that only   seems

to be dancing alone.

The call of the Sparrow

(RIP Brother)

I heard the Sparrow's call late in the night.
A mighty voice, it seemed, would come to play.
In harmony, our voices could take flight.

I knew of his sorrow, knew of his plight,
and even though his voice was tinged with gray
I heard the Sparrow's call late in the night.

In Sparrow's song I took such great delight
that in our songs, the darkness would decay.
In harmony, our voices could take flight.

His stanzas danced when bathed in holy light
and when the darkness loomed to hide the day
I heard the Sparrow's call late in the night.

Perhaps, in unison, we could ignite
some magic spark to keep the night at bay.
In harmony, our voices could take flight

Now, he sits on my shoulder when I write
for, in the end, his demons had their say.
I heard the Sparrow's call late in the night.
In harmony, our voices could take flight.

Clearly Wet

(A Romp of Otters)

A romp of otter splashes by
at play in crystal currents
that salve legs of the fisher
in his red-rubber riverpants

As free as they, he sees their play
through lashes of man
constrained by deeds and dollars
that never flow like water over stone
but trickle down late and short

Oh, play like those water-monkeys
man, play like you belong
beneath this laughing sun
enshrined in waters
that giggle all the way to
the sea

Free from the white noise
of bills and accolades, of wars
and superstitions, he dances a jig
as if the play is caught
in a smile as he takes up
the race for trout
with his furry fellows

with a slip, a splash, a guffaw
a fisherman is dunked
in clearer waters
than the preacher
knows

as the stream goes on

forever

But, in the garden

All the wars fade away at the gate
and best laid plans await
the rain from distant cloud

The corn knows no taxes
or bombs in distant lands
the beans grow ever faster
and flowers, born of sun
embrace the eye

In this place, only nature makes laws
and all the fond ingredients
are born by earth or sky

This verdant corner of my home
this deep and giving square
of loam resides outside
the hands of commerce
to remind my very soul
that the earth abides despite
the larger world
that does not reside here
in the special place
where I go
to hide

A New Freedom Song

(with apologies to Bob Marley)

We have bled for many kingdoms
and we've bled for many maps
while the kings, and all the generals
stayed behind to eat and nap

We have tilled a thousand crops
and built their mansions high
We have payed their many taxes
and sent our sons to die

But the kings, they never listen
to the cries of meekest men
they lie through soft pink faces
again, and once again

We have taken to the streets now
In the names of mercy and trust
To remind the rich and strong ones
that they have to listen to us

So I add my voice to freedom's song
and I raise my little sign high
as I march against their many wars
and I march against their lies

We are only workers and teachers
We are meek but unafraid
We denounce the newest fascists
and all the plans they've laid

'Cause the worker, he's a hero
and the mother, and the child
We are all the simple citizens
that the kings have so beguiled

Now the kings have had their riches
and the masters have had their day
'cause the meek are finally rising
and pulling feet from clay

to arise against the corporate man
and demand our slice of pie
to end the wars they perpetrate
and expose all the lies

So I sing to all the presidents
to the generals and other blights
That the time of change has come
to finally see the light

It's the meek who grow your food
and the meek who make your shoes
It's the meek who build your houses
and we've come to take our due

So I face your guns and badges
to sing my little song
and all my friends and neighbors
have come to sing along

All we ask is peace and freedom
and our little slice of pie
All we ask is peace and freedom
And our little slice of pie…

Three Times Lucky

(For Melissa Gayle)

I was born in a maze of maize and kindness
beneath such sun that love must surely sprout
and lacy drapes of clouds that weep with life.
The farmer's hands preached Genesis
as seeds were given up to womb of earth
and circles played out before the eyes
of the little germ that could.

I found a river-raised girl, a daughter
of the moon and author of life, a grail
of open arms, devoid of grief or shame
in such rich poverty that beans climb
the maypole like a stairway to heaven.
She entered me like a spring and
together, we laughed like a river
giggling over stones.

I read a poet that loves like this,
like a kiss freely given, like a lark
singing the day awake in a distant park
or an unrepentant limb, reaching
for the fire of another day.
To see her words at play
in the twisted sheets of love
denies the tears and fears
that shroud the gates
to bliss

to taste in those graceful words
a kiss, freely given.

Tears for Isaac

My grandson belongs
on the endangered species list
because his tribe forgot the gist of the
message of that shining queen, the sun.

The moon and her salty tides
abide in circles, and the tribes that forget
to honor the sky raise countless eyes to soot.

We forget that we, the bipedal citizenry
are but a flake on the grand mosaic
on a great blue ball so round that any
tail chased is tasted by tomorrow's tongue.

He belongs to the burgeoning mass
of a suicidal species, the authors of war
who burn the blood of dinosaur in the cauldrons
of commerce, who, with such fruited loins
purloin the gifts of earth to such excess
that our precious ball is sure to wobble.

But our mother grows angry
as if that lovely child's comrades are
but a virus on the precious skin of god

I hope that boy and his generation
can deny the greed that grandfathers taught
deny the wars their grandfathers fought
and shine beneath tomorrow's sun

but I fear the damage has been done...

Seasons

Spring

The first time was in a motel near
a river that flowed north near
a river that flowed south, so I
flipped her over halfway through

Summer

Oh dance of paisley and hope, of
unfettered breasts, the intimacy
of strangers well met, the dance
of strong legs, scissoring in the sun

Autumn

Oh, wife, oh love that so enlivens
the soul that the shell opens like
germinating seeds of wisdom to
light the throes of more than
simple friction explains

Winter

Oh crone, that so enflames the mind
what writhing grace awaits my later love
within the embrace that knows me well
and so shelters the kindest impulse
that Xanadu will fit me like a dream
of another life
with you

Riverman

But, I am made of water and stars, you see
and three orbs follow one to the other
devoid of need for various gods or incarnations

He was about those faces in the hieroglyphics
strewn about the sanctimonious winds
the flap of the prayer flags,
the thundering voice from crosses and mountaintops
stains of lamb's blood and currency
trappings of glamour, trapped
 in the many-spired cliffs of shame

in the uber-faced temples
in the judgment and clamor of priests
I sought some weathervane
but when they dunked me, I only heard the river
and my choir was populated by birds
that celebrated ALL FOUR winds
and the moon, that blue-blooded matron
moved in circles

The estuary became my tabernacle, that
salty mergence from whence I sprung
and would forever seek, that resting place
of rivers and dreams

I asked the pebble for the truth, made
my wish and tossed him into the pond
that feeds the stream of my consciousness
nodded, and followed his tracks

everywhere

Notes on the strength of grace

The hands of a hunter bend a bow
to pierce grandest heart of stag
but open, only love flies forth

*

Heroes are not washed in the blood
of war, but reflected in the peace
of a pond, in ripples flowing
into a low-hung moon

*

When the callused hands of the farmer
raise a daughter high, grandmothers
dance in the shade of strong arms

*

The sweating sharecropper and his mule
are titans; the landlord, a leech
and the woman in the kitchen
a fountain

*

I met a farmer, bent and humble
who feeds thousands of souls
and a king who starves many
for the price of his sculpted
glory

*

Kings are not
and rivers are not really borders
but taxis to the sea

Down the Spoon.

I wonder if her mind's eye will watch
As I paddle down the Spoon
Into my own epitaph
Through the gates to whatever
Xanadu awaits

That journey of a jejune soul
Into the guise of angels
Into the soil

I bid her no tears, no cause for
Melancholy or self-neglect, but a glimpse
Of paradise from the echoed eyes of love
Reflected on the smile of a face
That does not grieve
But watches the course
Of my last ride
Down the Spoon

Now and Then

Yesterday is an anchor
stuck in corrupt ooze
Tomorrow will never be
but, see, we are full of these
with nowhere for the moment
to play

outside, the vast, but in
the all-consuming clutter
of ifs, ands, buts, whens, awash
in ghosts and hyperbole
about what tomorrow will be
or not

and now, a lonely child

Second Sight

When one awakens each day
-      surprised   -
the very excess of summer
seems not warm, not quilt
but shroud, and maize, sweet corn
resembles dreams of cactus.

When the abyss is acknowledged
by the hourglass or the inextinguish
able fuse of disease, we see, you see
with the frightened eyes of futures
we must look forward for, absent
those feet

and that excess of pleasant climes
climbs the aged mind like ivy
on a university wall, like a call to arms
for sunbathers to see the harm in this.

Inevitable?

Perhaps our greed, our very thirst
for things, for diamond rings and
automobiles, dictates our fate like
a dinosaur comet, or a sun, peering
through a god's thin breath.

When tired eyes sparkle, wet
at the laughter of a child,
the elders try to forget
what the leaders
don't want
to know.

The Littlest Activist

rides his mother's shoulders like a cause,
like a victim, dangling from a corporate monster's jaws,
but, like a metaphor for hope, the light,
a thin, tiny voice, singing nursery rhymes in a world gone mad.

Glad tidings resound like the sight of a swan
gliding across the face of a lake
in a new sort of dawn.

Voices rise against the tide of bloated leeches,
"Won't you please come to Wisconsin"
we sing,
"for the help that you can bring"
we plead, in the seventy thousand songs
of mothers who baked the pies
we want a slice of.

Callused fingers raise slogans high
to quench the dragon's flame
to flip the game on the soft pink slugs
that usurp the pie for the table of the king on the hill.
We've had our fill of these, you see, these
money lenders and other thieves.

The inheritors of the world want mommies money
to buy lobsters and Cadillacs,
wants the teacher's bread to fill his head
with fine brandy and the screams of Muslims,
wants to pay for vast armies of mercenaries
with a little boy's future.

The monster wants to raise the army
to quiet the teacher, to quell the librarian,
to quiet the voice of one little boy,
and the president sits quietly by

The **horror...**

Ism

There is only what I see
but, see, the projector is only three inches
behind my three eyes, and
perhaps the tides, a million genocides,
the rise of sun, death of moon
are mine.

The things I taste, smell, the music I hear,
the breast I touch, and she, the soul that ravishes
nerve endings with everlasting concepts,
every singing sparrow, every sea,
every love, hate, every calamity
are but constructs of some corrupt me,
some synapse that spawns dervishes like these
to entertain some bloody god.

Oh, odd id that so condemns
his cohorts to hibiscus and doom,
that marries Gandhi and Hitler in some grand play,
that slays MLK to make room for Limbaugh
and flies the passenger pigeon to hell,
that grants generals the building blocks
of my universe
in some fit of pique;

I hope some other ism created this,
and I am but son of god, of sun, or a projectile
from the sum of another brain's projector,
a calculation of another mind,
otherwise –

what have I done?

Zen Garden

I am not nothing yet
with my carnival of deceits
my big red nose, my quest to fill
some large new womb with constructs
to fill a three-ring circus or a binder full of truth

I am so many lies
so many dank insecurities
that block the simple light of sun
as if to shroud the very glint of hope in fog
the membrane of my ism, the schism that keeps me

from everything

Newborn Fauna

I met Fauna in a scream
The very scream and pulse
Of insistent life, slippery
From the sacred sea

Two hands became
A father's hands, a shelter
From the sudden bustle
Of the world

While the weary all woman
Rested, the daughter
Of the moon sparkled
In eyes, forever opened

Mother of Pearl

Never mind the neon nights
the lights that brightened dancing days
of youth at play with love

Never mind the river
that carried you to me
or the others that held my
tiny dancer close
before I found my grail

Before I was ready to heal
you were there with the salve
the one svelte dancer
I was born to have

Our own dance is akin to wind
that touches our naked skin
just so, the mantra in the garden
that no one else knows

Our first shared breath
made of us a nation of souls
still at play in those paisley days
but holding the keys
to sacred sighs

the truth of us will be told
forever

in a garden sewn with love

Listen

Sometimes, you hear it with your spine
    the three-thousand mile chorus of whales
    the eyelash, impacting the sill behind the farmhouse sink
    the whump of dropping sun that caught her eye
    dozens of thousands of hooves in Zambia
    the wildebeest, zebra, elsewhere
    the squeak of leather on a draft-horse, bound to labor and woe
    the hush of snow on a Tibetan mountain, rustling prayer-flags

Sometimes, in your spine, you hear the crack of ancient whips
    You hear the mothers of heroes grieve
    for the children their children mutilated
    You hear the sun glint in the windows of the town
    the new-born town, catching the wink of sun
    the tumult of atrophied serenaders, dead singers
    the lizard king, crooning his slings and arrows
    the deep timpanic boom of doom,
    the song of a lark with a sky, a universe, full of room
    the serenade of the weaver, behind the loom
    the crescendo of a buisily breaking wave,
    the bite of the whip into yesterday's slave,
    the lament of a hermit in his cave

You wake to the boss-man's alarm, the yodel of a predator
    inglorious anthems, and the shame of dark pledges
    the industrial juxtaposition of clang and hiss
    the Dresdonian clash of oily whispers from the abyss
    but too,
    the sounds of bliss, the twining tongues of kiss
    a breath for the beleaguered lung
    songs sung to the nerve that connects one's mind to earth

Sometimes, with your spine, you hear the turbines
   the west wind that drives them into appliances
   in ranch-style homes with flapping flags
   and signs that extoll Texas high-school athletes

You hear lost speeches from dreamers and monsters
   lost gods, conjured from the lips of distant lovers
   the tuning fork of a hovering hummingbird
   the drum-beats of a thousand lost nations
   lost nations that knew the way to the moon
   lost sailors, screaming beneath the mother of waters
   lost innocence, parading itself on grimy streets
   sated thieves, rustling in wallets for small denominations
   the white noise that urges you to seek silence
   that whispering angel of nevermore
   the silent scream of the allwoman, bound to
   church and man, bound to fist and dollar
   bound to man with pearl and diamond collars
   bound to save us all in the guise of a crone
   that raises voice to kill our wars,
   that makes the choice to lead the peacocks that bound her to greed
   with the strident rightness of the grandmother song

The things you hear with your spine resound like a quiet harp
   like a carp, carved on your back with clean water and hibiscus
   like the weeping of a distant child, like the rain
   the viscous reminder of our mother's halotosis
   like the pain of the broken soldier, weeping
   beneath the overpass, Monsanto in the creek
   like the keening of first nations
   quieted beneath the churches' hobnail boot
   the jingle of their loot in the preacher's pocket
   a keepsake face, weeping in a locket

Oh, the sorrowful sounds that tingle your sweet core
   like the gauzy ministrations of Babylon's corporate whore
   the red glare of a colonial rocket, paving the way to hell

Hear the stampede of the centipede beneath the log
    the bark of the long silver dog pounding the pavement
    jammed with new beginnings, hope for distant days
    the cries of doomed hogs in slaughterhouse five
    when Dresden was still alive, the horror of hot blood streaming
    the voice of dead Bukowski, reciting gall in a California dive
    the gnashing teeth of the last man alive in Donner's pass
    the trumpet of a Parisian strumpet passing gass
    the murmur of furies, weeping for dead gods from Anne's grave
    the chattering of a homeless child's teeth in a cardboard cave
    the obscenely delightful tinkling trickle
    of eons-old ice melting into polar seas, the hissing hum of missing
bees
    the pleas for freedom in a corporate world

The things you hear this way are the very truth
    the metaphysical liberty bell, the sound of conscience
    the subliminal rapture of the spine, the quiet poems
    lurking between the spines of your mind's book
    the song you sing from the central nook of mind
    the kind of sounds that render mothers kind
    and open the book of fathers to pages of love
    the giggle of a million stars above the scurry of fools
    the swoosh of every tide to answer the call of moon
    the call of the Mississippi to smaller streams
    the call of the ocean to gather them, call of womb
    to answer every singing circle with sacred rhythms
    the whisper that tells us our leaders are not what they seem
    the laughter of a tumbling stream, the gleam
    of happy tears on a weary mother's cheek
    the music of imagined peace in a military regime
    the gunfire, implicit in every hungry flag unfurled
    the sun, herself, sighing in your daughter's curls
    the hymns of nature in an unnatural world

These are the things you can hear with your spine
    but in case your head drowns out the sound
    you can listen to mine

True North – Notes to a Muse

I lay abed, muse-ridden, last night's kiss
lingering, like verse under a ceiling
that looks for you - and the scent
on your pillow
sustains

sustains me like rain, like milk
from the breast of sky,
and the stride of your sylph's
hips map
my nation

The glint of diamonds, of stars
in the green sky of your eyes
dazzles - soft hands and deft hips
ignite long buried
sonnets

This trembling quill, this soft well
of noun and verb seek congress
with a muse that dances
with the moon

before the third eye
of a mere poet

Inside Out

(For Anne Sexton)

I enter the city like a prostitute
Or a cantaloupe with soft, dead seeds
Neon greases my eyes and the rain
Makes invitation to earthworms
To lubricate the grime inside
Something flicks, snicks open, a
A switchblade perhaps or a hunger
For a god to forgive me this

I didn't find nothing beneath the silks
Didn't find it below the cosmetics
It was not lurking in a blues bar, or the
Reunion of intruder and nectar of fruit-flesh
It wasn't in the Synagogue or the
Frenetic pulse of the rave, the
Pseudo circle of corrupted dance of
Bright ravens. I guess I lost it in the
Explosions of orgasms and Dresden

There is nothing in the forest, I know it
I know it in the song of brook, the warble
Of morning, the shriek of ravenous sun
But Jesus is a white guy on a redneck's wall
And God keeps manufacturing ammunition
The killdozers have run amok, the very forest
Gives way to ghettoes and diamonds for
The necks of Babylonian matrons in New York

I ply the forest with a flute, sit silent, chant
All oooooooming and shit, and at times I feel
Nothing wash me like a dutiful mother, like
A first kiss, like some sort of silent redemption
But something interjects itself like a fox
Like a rain that evaporates before it
Strokes the earth, and something comes
Crashing in

I try to write nothing, write it in a poem
Or a book, but my typer leaves an impression
And in love, nothing is seemingly temporary
I got on Jack's train, but nothing was not distant,
Not sitting in a Tijuana bar with a hooker
On its knee, not in a Chicago blues-bar or
Playing Frisbee on the commons at a liberal arts
College, not beneath a little plaid skirt or lurking
In the judgment of a priest, in a crusade
 Nothing, it seems is inaccessible

I am full of love, full of music and hope
Full of throbbing, yearning, full of fucking
Ambition and fear for my get, full of
Wanderlust and questions, full of
Snapshots and songs, full of
Love for a poet that sought nothing
In her garage, full of
Everything

Perhaps, nothing is just not
Out there

Valentine for a Friend

I have a friend that mends my words with grace,
that attended as those first verses stirred.
He taught me to wrap my phrases in lace,
to sharpen the images that I blurred.

He led me to a heart outside myself,
to write sun for a lady trapped in dark,
to wield my pen like a verbose elf,
to help her weary spirit fly like larks.

It is thanks to him that my sonnets fly
in the winds, the idiot winds of now,
that now and then my pointed pen complies
as if the sonnet's structure is my Tao.

 The poems that I write, the words I bend
owe much to the tutelage of my friend

Ghetto

There is a ghetto of the mind
A plague contained in the boxes of dim editors
That keep out the wholesome song of bard
The long limbed poem of the mind
The kind of verse that leaves Dick and Jane
Behind

There are hives of MFA hopefuls
Slinging empty words into dull ears
That chew at adjectives like the haunches
of dry matrons, that eschew stronger songs
of loud retort to modern claims
that poetry be free of meaning

Never mind the tidy poem about the chair
Sing to me in paint and fury the story of the ass
Never mind the patriotic drivel
Festoon my ears with the cry
Of children broken over the knee of war
The whore that knows no other way
Man's wildest dervish
Let out to play

Erupt this mindful ghettoes' walls
With fountains of words from an untidy stream
Of consciousness beyond the thrall
Of the editor's call for tripe
The time is ripe to answer the poetic heroes' call
For something so beyond the tiny expectations
Of tiny minds that poets set the very sky afire
Like Allen did with "Howl"

Too many broken victims
Too many women harmed
To many lively wars
Too many shrieking alarms
Too many bloody heroes
In a slowly poisoned world
Too many triumphant generals
With gory flags unfurled
Too many asphalt ghettoes
Reeking of martial law
Too many silent voices
Beneath the monster's paw
Too many starving children
Too much topsoil gone
From man's collective lawn

We've spawned the verse of hypocrites
Who write of nothing much
In times that test the poet's pen
But it is time for real wordsmiths
To rise in the time of empty words
In the clutches of sterile surgeons
To once again sing a strident and demanding
Refutation of the monsters
To lend our quills to greater tasks
Than the boxes of journals allow
To break free of that ghetto of the mind
And write outside those grimy walls
To light a brighter flame
To plant kernels of truth deeper
Than the pages of academic journals –

It is time, dear poet

To howl again

Another Song

We dance to waltz, to rhythms tried and true
to bind our feet to music bound in love,
and arrows from the bow that cupid drew
ring out like the gentle song of doves.

The voice of the poet follows the waltz,
as words and silent music seem to merge.
There are lovers and flowers to exalt,
virtues to extol, stories from the verge.

And oh, these stories, sung in tones of hope
delight the ear, but bound to beat of moon
are seen by some to bind their voice with rope,
to restrict one's voice to one simple tune.

They spew their poems in unruly rows
as songs beyond the borders are composed.

The bards of old would surely roll in graves
to hear the howl of words so unrestrained
from those who don't see words as structure's slaves.
New songs are sung with freedom's sweet refrain.

Women writhe in the light of open words,
moistened in the grasp of the pioneer
that does not bask in some poetic herd,
but shouts the truth with a snarl and a sneer.

Multi-colored phrases, shrouded in mist
of metaphor challenge the mind to find
the essence of obtuse fables, the gist,
the sound of the drum, the taste of a kiss.

Wrapped in freedom's open hand, I believe
I'll write with my heart
on a black leather sleeve.

Into the Out

There is medicine in the boreal forest
in the chanting streams, the voice of
water over stone, the whisper of wings.
There is a moment of clarity when a man
marks a one way path from in to out,
an immersion in a stream of consciousness
more literal than the shallow pond of gods.

There is a metaphorical tearing, ripping
shredding sound as titles and contracts
give way to the aroma of the very moment.
The forest seems to sigh as haunches ply
the paths devoid of concrete and shame.

I, (and I am all I have, so I will write me
gently, with no apology to academics
with sterile pens in soft hands,) took this
path with an ark, a river, a sky, full of robust
companions. And such a world revealed
itself to me that my eyes danced, my ears
heard songs to scorn any anthem.

And so, the forest is my nation, and I
but a citizen of the real, hiding from
maps like the tiniest waterfall.
It is not moot that a river is born
beneath my garden, or that I will
lie here forever, not moot that my
song resounds from a simple
wooden flute, with a loon
singing along to tell me
I belong.

Only Rob

I am only this
a mad glad fool who hides
between words strewn on the
battleground of peace,
the man with the least in the
kingdom of more, a whore
on the field of commerce,
a flute-song in a busy sky, a lover.

But I am a wordslinger
who sings the undercurrent of love
in Dodge City, in Babylon, in Dresden,
the voice of the forest
in a city of doom,
a brother to all as war looms
in the hearts of generals, priests
and other miscreants.
I am a mural of nature's grace,
out of place in the vivisection
of the American dream, contraband.

I am only a grandfather, a gardener
who weeps at the sight of the future.

A Momentary Lapse of Reason

Now does not make promises or plans
does not seek apostles or acolytes

If the turgid tit of today does not please
the sheep bleat lies of tomorrow or
legends of evermore

Better to suckle at this point of Earth's
areola, this holy dot in circle's path
than to waste now painting gods
on mirrors

Broken Belles

Oh my broken belles,
you courtesans from the dark side
of paradise, what dear plagiarisms,
what specters tarnished your lights,
what dismal sights did dreams bestow?
What furies drove you so?
The belles that pealed so brightly
shine yet in the bell jar of my mind,
shine yet in line and phrase that raised
my sights from the soil to the very womb
of a universe we hide too deep,
to the tombs of those who bled
those lines that haunt me still,
the lines that resound in deepest sleep.
I drink of their chalice of sorrow
that I may carry on to write tomorrow,
to write my way from dark to light
with three broken larks flying in a mind
that will not succumb to abyss or
gnash at bits of burning soul,
not give in to the lure of death
but rise above the murk
of interior decay
to sing
to ring
to dance
another day…

Oh lass, that wields a poet's pen,
if you must give your heart to men,
hold tight to spirit's burning light
lest the hands that hold you near
lead you into darkest night.

The light, you see, stems not from those
who harness you when they propose,
but from your heart, your poetry,
your prose.

Never mind the man behind the curtain.

Thanks

(With apologies to William Burroughs)

Thanks, Uncle Sam,
for fencing in the noble savage,
for the dead buffalo, the poisoned wolves,
and all those stop signs,
signs of progress, surely.

Thanks for the slow thick rivers
and the shivers, gazing at the Monsanto
fetuses in Vietnamese jars, and the lost
eyes of our warriors
Thanks for horror.

Thanks for cement, high rents,
our large automobiles and
silicone wives,
for the plants of ants, printing monopoly
money to equip more soldiers
with bullets and dead conscience.

Thanks for Michael Jackson
and the tea-baggers faction,
the new John Birch in the lurch
towards imagined freedom.

Thanks for making god angry
and letting us build his bombs.
Thanks for Arlington,
and the symbolism of fireworks.
Thanks for Hunter Thomson's gun.
Thanks for fun with Dick and Jane,
Thanks for fucking Spot.

Thanks for Caddilacs.
Thanks for the Knack of making enemies
and the burial of pesky facts.
Thanks for Fox News.
Thanks for all the vitriol you spew
from pulpit to pew,
from the wealthy few to the
sheep that they fleece to
hang blood diamonds from chicken necks,
from the big white house to the
poor louse that built it.

Thanks for hair-spray,
for toy guns and John Wayne.
But thanks, most of all for

Texas.

The horror…

Water

As a citizen of the
Upper Mississippi watershed
Atop the great divide
I run north to escape
The tide of Tide
And Monsanto's twisted
Fetuses

The branch below the hill
Looks North with watercress
With brookies and hope
That corporations will not
Piss in my well
But we are many
Like bison ghosts
Like our first-nation hosts
And we shit in the bottom
Of the chalice
As the blue planet
Browns

Not a poem

This is not a poem about the war machine
not about gore strewn sand or the whore of
Babylon, not about daffodils or dew
This poem does not sing anthems or psalms
does not warble like a singer drunk on pina
coladas beneath the shade of palms, does not
offer alms to the poor or open doors to
greater consciousness, does not preen
like Billy Collins on public radio or
try to glean a ride in the academic pushcart
Nope, this is only a playground for words
an unruly usurper of phrases better left
to the apothecary of the mind-bender
the mortar and pestle of the wordgrinder
with a metaphorical monkey gibbering
for treats from a confused crowd
that embraces a loud and expletive-filled
rant about nothing much at all
This is nothing more than a literary fall
from grace, an excursion to a place of
infinite grace, a place left in the light
of whimsy where the long anguish
of Baudelaire, the endless night of Poe
are lost to the mercy of aimless nouns and
verbs, to the verbiage of poetry's miscreants
those lovers who are not harnessed to the rose
but to the sultry slut in fishnet hose
This is the advent of gleeful nonsense
the birth of a new bohemian rhapsody
chanted by a fool in a redrubbernose
the giggling gibberish of those to whom the language
is but a redrubberball, the balderdash
that spills from the cracked skull of a twisted
mind, a mindful attempt to write about
nothing, nothing much

This is not a poem after-all

The Apocalypse of the Vanities

Oh lust, that resists the uterus to seek gold,
to draw maps in blood, to bleed the earth
to fuel Cadillacs with Viagra and oil, to shave
the genitals of woman to resemble thin waif,
to split atoms in the names of mirror gods
and so spill the blood of innocents that rivers
coagulate.

Oh, ego, superego, uber-ego that drives us
down the clearly marked path to ruin, what
hunger is too heinous for the loins of man
to cherish; what desire too dark for the
kings and clerics to perpetuate?

Oh, bloody spear, oh, darkest metaphor,
what tribe is too remote for your self-faced gods,
for your currency, and soft hungry merchants?
What cataclysmic clap is too severe for misanthropes
that simply must blow shit up?

Oh, scientist, in your red and white smock,
what monster is too hungry for you to unleash?
At what age is the corporate leader too old
to sharpen?

Oh god, in your temples and sharp spires, how
many tribes must sublimate their sun, their rain
for the empires of your fathers, how much blood,
how many languages, how many circles must die
to dim the sight of stars with a mirror's face?

Plastic Francewater bottles grace the face of earth
and squadrons of ants scurry everywhere
in contrails of soot that poison a blue stone's breath.
A war criminal gets a new heart while a twenty
year old student of philosophy dies, and the lives
were weighed in their measure of gold.

If only bullets were crafted of gold.

Orwell had no idea.

This is the strenuous bleat of the lamb, the bullets
of the wordslinger that spits truth like the vomitus
of the weeping altar boy, the broken first nations,
the lover in an eon of rape, the screams of Hiroshima,
the weeping hymen of the moon, the singer of the
silent river's song.

As rivers die and dreams of peace subside,
some of us sing brighter songs than anthems
or hymns of great crusades. Some of us
bleed LOUD in terms of such reproach
that sleeping sheep awake.

Won't you sing along?

February

winter
    drips
    from
    eves

stalactites
      reach
      for
      the
      spring

with arms full of sun

Punctuation

I learned to punctuate in Mexico City.
I learned that extremity is the mother
of immortal phrase from a crazy writer.
He gave me back my explosions, mayhem,
the unexpected emphasis of retort.

He basked in the company of poets
beneath the warm poppy's blanket
where nouns wrestled in the nomenclature
of heroes and misbegotten dervishes.

He led me to a church.
He led me to a church hand in hand
with a ghost in a sun-dress.
She said her name was Joan.

This writer of kaleidoscopes of laughter
and angst, of twisted words and the quasi-
holy hieroglyphics of the over-revving mind
showed me the most lovely horror to twist
the very nation of love beyond any notion
of borders, any fences of reason.

William Burroughs taught me to punctuate
when he formed that perfect period
with a bullet.

When the Wordfather Rises

(for Jim Dunlap)

young poets sing as larks –
synapses crackle with sparks, and the page is lit!

(by your hand, again, and again)

A gentle hand raises fledglings aloft with a touch
as soft as a reader's eyes, that language may fly.

When the sun alights on a sprout and encouragement
falls like rain, the pain of exposure gives way
to exuberant sonnets, to verses of hope that
dance like jesters and saints from leaf to leaf,
from sheaves of verses that curse the dark
as the wordfather rises to sponsor growth.

Oh, godfather of my wee voice, rise again
to help the clumsy colt to run like four winds,
to build a ladder to scenes of shores untracked
by hobnail boots of the false editor, the wizened
academics that preach, "Show, don't tell,
write like me; the trees are green, the roses, red -
we've made our bed of innocuous words
and the time of painting with adjectives is dead."

You taught me to build a magic bench, to
build a stream to carry a fragile boat to a shining sea,
to be the poet that my mind's eye sought to be.

You taught me to build a bridge of words
to lead from misery to the very shore of glee,
to be unafraid of the powers that be, to fling
words of peace into the very maw of kings.

You taught me that language is a magic thing,
a mighty thing, that a spear of words may penetrate
the very heart of war, and release the heart

of a warrior to sing.

We need our mentors more than ever now,
now that the brows of those kings knit blankets
of innuendo to cover the earth with maps of blood.

We need you to sharpen our pens, again, and again,
even as you grow weary of this battle of words,
lest our voices grow unheard to herds of sheep,
lest we reap what the academics sew, and our
wordslingers be contained in the tiny box
where Dick and Jane languish, in reams
of obscene mediocrity, lest the flow
is lost on the shore where saplings
fear to grow.

In your name, I write three hundred poems a year,
in your name, I put my fears aside, buy a ticket,
take the ride across vistas of words, unafraid
to fling the truth at the powers that be,
unafraid to rhyme, to flow like the beats of old,
to sing the boldest songs of peace
that my meager pen can bestow
on the eye of any reader,
to broach the armies
of wealth with
the truth,
to lead the next young poet
to books that the future
needs to read.

Equinox 2

I arrived on the cusp
with the equinox
and I wear so many skins
behind my caul

September and I are not
summer or fall, not
vicious or kind, not
static

but everything
and nothing at all

Digging up Buddha

Today, I dug up Buddha
to place him where he could
look out over the last forest,
the last prairie, and remembered
finding Jesus, hanging
from the rafters in his garage,

and I pondered the shared
symptoms of mortality I have
in common with this rough little
house, this forest, this planet,
and though I didn't plan it,
I began to feel god-like
in my slow concurrencies
of choking, as if death is only
a grand and mutual graduation
to end all but one run on sentence…

Organic

We are organic that entwine
with the motion of sweetest breeze
We are music that sing ourselves
with one shared rhythm
When I follow my muse from
the arch of your foot to
the muscle of thigh, to
the home of your deepest sigh,
the earth itself becomes my church
and you, my connection to the sky

We are kin to stars and soil
and when we dance to love's decree
we flow like a river, bound
for the sea - our mingled breaths
paint the very wind with a
jubilant soliloquy

Sky-clad lovers, in tune with the
earth, we writhe, in turn, with magic
and mirth, joined in the union
of two souls, climbing the stairway
of sensation to the tune of
procreation, safe in the arms
of a perfect circle

We are holy when the moon
has her way with us

Ohio

My innocence died at Kent State
when Sam went to war against peace.
I came to the battle quite late
when innocents fell to the beast.
I understood that war breeds war,
that revenge is a poisoned dish,
and blood never evens the score.
I HEARD Country Joe and the Fish.
I finally learned to give a damn,
to forsake expansionist goals.
I wouldn't be goin' to Viet Nam
or be filling a hero's hole.

When I picked up that first bullhorn
a soldier for peace was born...

Love at First Sight

My second birth was not
smeared with any lamb's blood,
but witnessed by blue beat of moon
and neon's bold refrain

I won her from Joker
on a battleground of red felt
and hard maple swords

I saw my future, my grail,
in the eyes of a midnight
blond

Breathe
(for Marc Creamore)

Grip that tractionless wind and drag it in
   with the glee of hopscotch sounds,
   the cadence of hearts, scent of
   rotten apples, deeper, deeper.

The leather is cracked on the bellows, but
   bellow you must, as a real poet is not
   but a whisper when kings march
   sheep to the slaughter.

When your very ribs become unyielding cage
   and the truth rattles like rusty spokes,
   it is in the speaker to rave, to persist
   in flutesong and diatribes, however short.

Air is god, you see, and hard to come by.

Blow it out, all of it and more, blow with
   that pursed O until the graveyard is
   expelled, with expletives for tyrants
   and quaking love songs for her.

Release the dogs of war to light of day
   that their shadow does not fall on another
   generation of children at play, but dies
   in the maelstrom of kindly evolution.

Force your tired lungs empty of yesterday
   that there be room for the hope of tomorrow,
   for poems uttered to an enlightened world,
   for moonbeams where the sky was dark.

Air is god, you see, and sacred things
   don't always come easy.
Breathe, good brother –

   just breathe…

Notes to a Dying Child

Yesterday, you were scabby-kneed and adventurous -
fearless in your small bright world
Cricks were for splashing in, after frogs, after minnows,
after breakfast.

Yesterday, you lived like an insect, drawn to light
and never mind the burn.
Wars were on the television and funerals were secrets
that babysitters ate popcorn through
and father was a roof.

Yesterday, (or was it last week?)
you were an innocent lover
that schemed to enter the cotton playground
that waited for a brown-eyed pirate -
never mind a roof.
Rain was for dancing in and thunder was joyous noise.
The grail became a sigh.

The bombs dropped closer and funerals had dead heroes.
The cotton sent magic rhythms to erect antennae
as dancing grew purposeful.
You were a roof, and insects swarmed beneath you.
Through it all was she, your community,
the only government you needed -
and still, the cotton drew you true North
to the tide, as time accelerated like Hunter's red convertible
and the moon made of you-
a hero.

Dancing slowed as war reached out for insects.
Light sprouted fire and the grail disappeared in the smog.
Your legs grew so very long.
Now, you sing shorter songs and funerals leak
through the roof that sags beneath the weight
of a larger sky, and words are too slow

to patch it.

Perhaps, tomorrow, those insects will forgive you
for making the world so big, the rain so warm,
but for today, the time has come to bury you, dear boy,
beneath gray hair and the ponderous weight of time.

I'm sorry the hourglass leaked like the roof.

Dancing with the Moon

She lies like a universe at dawn,
alone, but he is there

She describes tighter circles
like planetary fingers
circling sun

His absent whispers brush her
in the quickening of day

Snow speaks in a hush
against the pane, translucent
as secret skin

As night gives way to light
he is there, somehow
as she dances with the moon

Notes from a different flute

I play notes from a different flute, you see, a flute
    that mimics the loon, and knows no anthems.

*
*
*

I saw dawnlight play across a breast, and supped
    at the apothecary of the moon, was cured
    of green ambition, save that which stained
    the dungarees of a simple gardener.

*
*
*

I wilt, annually, at the rocket's red glare, squint
    against the fire of Hiroshima, and wonder
    why heroes are crafted of killers, why
    Farmer John is not named like them,
    why a dirty uniform is not honored
    to a higher degree than a bloody one.

*
*
*

We teach our children to behave when we are not -
    hAve, that is, in our pursuance of large borders,
    homes, entrancer screens, bazillionaire boys,
    playing at gladiator games - bloodsport in the sun,
    large automobiles, breasts, wars, vast, ignoble gods
    shaped like bankers from fallible civilizations,
    crumbling beneath the scientist's weapons.

*

I look at the old plow, left beside the fence, sans funeral
and I wonder if my poems, my pleas, are but rust.

*
*
*

A national symbol gnaws at carrion at the edge of a concrete
river, beak covered in gore, and I wonder why Al
thinks currency will mop up his oil spills..
Hillary and Sarah run so fast, so far, and I wonder if a fool
and a criminal, are really the best representatives
of Venus on a wobbly planet, prone to testosterone
and mayhem, or just disguised residents of Mars?
Patti, Maya, Ani, Gwendolyn, sing so softly now, unheard
in the din of bombs and Martian ambition.

*
*
*

My truck is twenty-one years old, but it still runs, while
our grandchildren play sedentary games before
machines that do their thinking for them,
playing gladiator games before a bloody
screen, while fireflies remain unchased.

*
*
*

Let me play a happy song, a voice of Peregrine falcons,
nesting on the noxious cliffs of New York,
in defiance of Wall Street and the Mayor
that bought the highest seat in town,
a voice of tomorrow's children, singing
in spirals 'round a distant Maypole,
a voice of wind whispering through the arms
of the last old growth pines, perched at the verge
of the mother of waters, the song of a lark.

*
*
*

I go to funerals, and funerals, ever more funerals,
    as the last flower children wilt, as Allen is dead
    and funerals for poetry are published by the likes
    of Billy Collins, and Charles Simic, funerals
    bereft of starving children, dying planets, or song.

        I mourn Walt most of all.

*
*
*

I sit in church, where the Sioux River splits granite,
    listening to the chorus of cymbals and bells,
    but the river runs away, ever away, as if
    it knows I am a son of the man that rapes her.

*
*
*

The clothes dance on the line, to song of Northwind,
    less hollow somehow, than when they are worn
    by pink creatures with mirror-gods, singing,
    dancing with serpents and judgment.

*
*
*

The coyotes and wolves sing so sweetly, and we, the
    purveyors of doom, the predators most high,
    yet sing as well, rarely, but in fine voice.
While tanks tread on the innocent, tractors plant corn.
While urbanites consume, germination is fostered by
    a gardener, the rain yet cleanses us, and the
    river still gathers itself to harmonize with a flute.

        Perhaps, after all, it is not too lateto hear the music...

Precipice

The boy chased fireflies
on nights he could hear the corn grow -
grew cards in spokes,
and Shouted "CAR!"
for timeout until the white cotton
called.

The young man loved
like a dervish, battled monsters
with placards and daisies.
He rode an iron horse into
the dynamo of time to find
her.

The father loved like a woman
who knows that the gyroscope
must slow in the face of
monsters, must
warm the children in gentle arms, must
understand that heroes
do not kill other father's
progeny.

The grandfather loves a crone
and a slower dance in step
with the silent sigh of moon.
He loves like a patient river
that nears vast brine.

Today, they dance together
celebrating reunion
at the precipice.

Notes from a Nighthawk

(Circa 1975)

Hey Stony, got any boy 'n' girl?
ain't good for the baby, but momma
gots to git well, gots to pay the man
gots to git in ol' John's pocket, baby

Hey Stony, did you hear 'bout fat Rita?
she hit a hot-shot, man, faded out
like the settin' sun man, they found her
cat eatin' her face, behind the bakery there

Hey Stony, my man be out come Friday
how 'bout a little taste, brother, just to
like hold me over, cause he'll be
servin' you know, over by the avenue

Hey Stony, what'd that doctor say?
Yeah, man, that fuckin' Monsanto done
fucked up a whole lotta boys, y'know?
Dude, what she say when you wake up -

all screamin' an' shit, all, like crazy?
Oh, sorry, man, I didn't know
yeah, yeah, it's probly for the best
You shouldn't have hit her Stony

Hey Stony, Howlin' Wolf is in town
I know you white boys love them blues
Yeah, man, best take that booger-sugar
you know how them weekend hippies be

Hey Stony, did you hear 'bout Slim?
Yeah, man, straight-razor
Life's a bitch, then some fool
cut yer throat wit a razor
that's it

Paisley and Napalm

I was smitten by the unfettered breasts
and the smoke that swirled around in my head.
But our leaders had failed a basic test
and our patriots were coming home dead.

Paisley and napalm filled the very air
with riots of color and vast fire.
Stars in my eyes, and flowers in my hair
drew the ire of my straight-laced sire.

Abbie, Kerouac, Ginsberg, led the way
with kaleidoscopic words of delight,
but the tricky dick wanted us to fight,
to give our bright blood to a distant fray.

We gave our blood in Ohio instead,
and saved our passion for music and love
while our brothers, our cousins, screamed and bled.
They embraced the pentagon, we, the dove.

The poets back then wrote words for a cause
as opposed to today's empty verses.
Our queens danced in circles and burned their bras
while peaceniks were met with clubs and curses.

The revolution is dead: we sold out.
Our poets, it seems, have all been neutered.
The poets of Naropa, so brightly tutored
have forgotten how to howl, how to shout.

Another war has bloomed, bloody and long,
and again, our poets must fight with songs.

Notes from an object lesson on shame

THANKS FOR THE SHAME, DAD!
THANKS FOR THE SHAME, PRINCIPAL JONES!
with your slab of wood named "the whistler"
for all those three/quarter inch holes to make it sting.
I think of you each time my pants meet my shoes,
each time I sport a bruise.
THANKS FOR THE SHAME Mrs. SEIGLER!
for recognizing a fine young mind
and beating the luster off with a yardstick
and that spittle that punctuated your fine screech.
THANKS FOR THE SHAME, FATHER JOHN!
for the weight of god and the nightmares.
THANKS FOR THE SHAME, DAISY!
I never wanted to go to college anyway.
*I **wanted** to work in a factory, **wanted***
*you to kill my son, **wanted** to carry him in scars.*
THANKS FOR THE SHAME, UNKLE SAM!
you bad-ass motherfucker,
for the orange, the crispy critters, for years of blood,
for necklaces of ears, the tears of multicultural
mothers and the culling of the poor, for
thinning out those young black men,
for lining pockets of deferment boys with cash
for freedom and a grateful nation, AMEN!
THANKS FOR THE SHAME, Mr. PRESIDENT!
for crowning Zionists with dead Muslims,
and making our corporate masters so wealthy:
my children don't really need health-care anyway.
THANKS FOR THE SHAME, JESUS!
for making me be the one to find you,
for making me five minutes late to cut the rope,
for the creaking sound I still hear after 30 years.

ThANKS, MOTHERFUCKERS, for all this weight,
for the oily coils of shame I strain against,
for night's greasy sheen of ghosts, for this

armor, unpierced by hope, for the tools
to deal with the hungry necromancer of
reality and screams, for dire days
in the kingdom of blind sheep
and broken lives, the bleating
of lemmings.

Thanks for the slippery salve of shame, everybody:
I'll use it to oil my guns.

The Chair

An empty chair rides a weathered porch
on a night dark as Baudelaire's flowers.
Another poet has passed the verbose torch.

He rocked out there for countless hours,
nursing nouns and verbs to dance like lovers,
to salve society; to throw the truth at power.

While children slept beneath their covers,
he fought monsters with verses of words,
and around that old chair, a poet still hovers.

From milk of human kindness, he made curds
as if the gist of wholesome thought grew cheese.
He made the simplest phrases fly like birds.

He wrote of love and gentle folk of the land,
of miracle of rising sun, of generosity, and bliss,
but society showed him the back of its bloody hand

and his last verse floated away on pink mist.

Owed to a Window Bird
(For Julian)

To fly so high, and drill so deep
must a sparrow craft a bed of words -
of diamonds for his friends to keep.
I heard them, my brother, I heard.

Must a sparrow craft a bed of words
before a window freezes flight?
With highs and lows forever blurred,
your tiger burned so fucking bright!

Before a window freezes flight
a man made stanzas dance like stars
that twinkled with a magic light.
In nations of words, you became a Czar.

A man made stanzas dance like stars -
twisted them into brilliant rhymes.
I think perhaps, you wrote from Mars,
with muse from dark to most sublime.

Must a poet craft a bed of words
to live forever in our eyes?
I'll always see you as a bird,
flown aloft, in eloquent skys

Dreams of Nothing

nothing
is the color
of ancient bones
and books as yet
to sing -

of the lotus
on an imagined pond

Water's Leap

Now, it seems the clearest suicide.
The Bad River leaps off the cliff
as if it knows what dire flavors
lie in wait miles and weeks below.

My mother's veins are shot full
of evolutionary cyanide.
Gravity will claim these waters,
replace trout with carp; with
garbage; with coagulated
junk food.

The lexicon of water over stone
will give way to voices of shit;
to the ooze of sludge words,
mud words, words that must
wear boots against the future.

It leaves my legs to find those
of oil-rigs in a salty gulf.

It makes me want to leap.

Undertow

I read the daily paper
Watched the television
Booted up the puter
And the reek of carrion
Infused another Monday
I tried to swim to dancing
To song, to children's
Smiles, but the undertow
Led back to Poe
I heard the gunshot on
Public radio
Perhaps Dr. Gonzo
Was right

The Big Rock Candy Mountains

 I want to write my way to the Big Rock Candy Mountains,
to the fountain of youth, to sylvan streams, to the uncouth
freedom of Xanadu. I don't much care for present reality,
an' ain't got nuthin' better to do. I want to write a world
free of misery or war, a world where eagles soar in un-
tainted skies, where my eyes can spy Sam's albatross, aloft
in blue. I want to construct a verbose geography of verse
where the curse of war lifts like morning fog, and the dogs
of war return to mind the bleating sheep.

In the Big Rock Candy Mountains, the streams run clear,
they're chock-fulla' fish and the hills are full of deer.
We'll have nothing to fear from our neighbors, and our
labors will result in heavy crops of food. Multi-colored
broods'll smile like light on lakes, shine like the vast
wedge of Orion, like the ocean full of milky way, sing like
loons on a lake filled with silver. Every morn will wake
with rising hope, take away dread when children quit their
beds to scatter seed for chickens, scatter laughter like rain.

I'm building the Big Rock Candy mountains in my head.
I'm building Xanadu, and I'm making room for you. Our
beds'll be stuffed with feathers; two pillows for every
head. The weather'll be like it usta was, and everyone well
fed. I'll be yonder, waiting, two dreams west of setting sun,playing a
maple fiddle, ten minutes after I'm dead. I hope to see you there,
someday, in the Big Rock Candy Mountains.

Seven Shades of Gray

(With apologies to Ted Hughes)

One is a wolf
That circles my bones like a moon
An avid reader of checkmarks
On a rusty bucket
List

Another is a sky like a factory floor
Greasy with poisons and weight
That presses like god's foot
My throat is raw with this

Fingers of oaken sentinels
Pry at the sky as if to redeem sun
From that kingdom of lead
Or to unleash unbidden rain
That loosens such grand feet as theirs
As the last tears of color fall

The gloss of obsidian has left my ink
Like the last pullet
In the jaws of a mink
And my stanzas sob like broken children

The lake absorbs bleak furies
That lash at hope like teeth of iron
And the only voice from above
Speaks in the dialect of thunder
I wonder what I would look like
Written on granite

The evening news is painted thus
With wars enough for all of us

And rainbows absorbed by greed
The frogs are resting in coal-dust-mud
And I can gain no purchase
On the thin breath of god

Soot falls like pollen from some
Long dead flower
That wilts in mankind's final hour
To repose beneath a slab of stone,
Colorless and cold   proclaiming
suicide

The White Side of the Ball

The light comes before the thunder
and in that interval twixt sparkle and boom,
I live.

There be songs at play as ice forms
on bearded faces that moisten
northwind with fountains
of story, storms
that feed the land.

There are angels with swords of fire
and floods that carry seeds
to hungry soil.

Never mind the pit, the swinging steel,
the hiss of its nearing: it is merely
the metronome that keeps the time
while I sing.

The Black Side of the Ball

Various and sundry demons
learn my secret names, writhing
on the thunder-vine that
connects the very of me
to some semblance of cave.

Oh, I roam the light yet
like some not-ghost, some
hollow deity brought to life
by some monster in a mirror,
some razor-haloed miscreant,

but that yellow orb is mocked.

What light may ignite clarity
in a shadow bereft of pit's comfort?

What mere flute peals with the bass
of vast stones grinding me
a soft new home, sealed somewhere
between the thunder
and hell?

The jingle of finger cymbals
is moot, it seems, on the lips
of a chasm

.

Propaganda

"Re-examine all that you have been told...
dismiss that which insults your soul."

Walt Whitman

Read this, the propaganda of my loins,
   the very electrons of wrinkled dynamo –

"Fuck a whole bunch of generals and kings,"
   lest your get be blessed with endless
   war, buried beneath mounds of papers
   denoting their servitude; paper devoid
   of poetry or love's lubrication.

Ignore the rants of men who would be king –
   by seeking thrones, they announce
   themselves unworthy of those seats.

Defeat the warlords by the vision of your backs
   as they cannot attack your brothers,
   denied the blood of your sons to
   propel their grandiose schemes.

Dreams of freedom are not solidified by war,
   but dissolved by the blood of misspent
   youth, buds, harvested prior to the
   bloom of any wisdom to come.

Resist the pull of magnetic generals to slaughter.
Desist in accepting the notion that other men
   must be bent to the tasks of your king,
   and insist that your leader proclaim peace,
   releasing your cubs from the filthy bonds
   of war, and smile on your fairest arbiters.

True heroes stand tall against such dirty deeds,
   forsaking the bomb for the plow, feeding
   nations of brothers, regardless of their names

for god or the waste of their cathedrals,
the strong and callused hands that will not
kill the spawn of one for the profit of another
and so deny the circles of sun and moon,
but hold the future dear in dirty hands,
the men who know that the land is god
like them, like flowers and mothers,
that know that those who claim knowledge
of god make these claims to dark purpose.

When a journey calls to your feet, keep it small
lest you feed the inferno that burns us so.
Down the hill, near the creek, there is a place
beyond the value of distant lands, a vista
that lives just beyond your point of view,
but closer than the one that jets bestow
on the eyes of globetrotters that forget
the land beyond their own back yard,
a nearby garden to feed the soul that needs
not giant's eyes, but merely small steps.

The base of the rainbow is behind your eyes,
waiting for the man who knows he is not
privy to everything, no miner of fool's gold,
but a lover of small riches, who needs not wealth
to thrive, but only love and daily bread,
a man alive to simple provocations, open
to the full flavor of meek notions.

Never mind the machine behind the curtain, the
entrancer who tries to fill you with a need
for baubles, large shiny objects made by slaves
in distant lands to fill the hands of the idle,
the reeking president that wants your children's
blood to build larger maps for Jesus, amen,
the academic that tries to take away your adjectives,
the dumb bitch, chanting, "Drill, Baby, Drill."
the numb accountant, the man that tells you
what god wants you to do, the white hooded artist
that says he knows what the right color is –

fuck 'em all; think for yourself.

Bones

These are my bones that the future may read
As epithets from a subconscience short of sand
That illuminate dark recesses of commerce

This is my breath that grates at good moods
In the nomenclature of dead soldiers
And the Dodo, the hush of absent snow

These poems that rattle from my spines
In dusty cathedrals of word and marble
Beseech peace in the name of love

When flesh fails to encumber me and time is not
I'll be dancing on the shelf beside big gay Allen
Awaiting fingers to ply my sighs, to leap at phrase

Perhaps, when the bombing stops, they will read
The echoes of a tired lover, the psalms of a man
Who loved like a woman in the hours of war

These are my bones

To Whisper like a Dragon

(For my heroes)

Poets should not be mirrors, but necromancers,
jugglers of emotional geography
and the landscape of the human heart.

This art of ours is moot if one is faint of that
great muscle that measures each stanza,
each turning of tide, that gentle metronome
which tells us that the earth abides.

This craft of granting language flight, this song
of fluid rhyme, of the conscious paring of words
to pry open closed eyes to birth of light
so delights the reader that nations, eons
weep at the plight of an oily bird.

We write thus to be read by a distant future,
for that is the purpose of the poet.
A vast responsibility ensues when we posture
for posterity in our gardens of verse.
This, then, is the curse of our tribe.

Whisper we must, with feathers in our pens,
of love, of water over stone, of flowers,
but again, and yet again, we must decry
the cost of war, the misery of our fellows,
for then, my friends, we are poets.

The body electric demands that we howl
at the bloody king, that we illuminate monsters
with the strongest light of nomenclature,
that we anoint the heart with warmest oil
and toil to slay dragons that roam hallowed halls,
to shout FIRE! in a burning room and point
nouns and fingers at the monster with the match.

If Rome is ever burning, and the peaceful child
of any god is torn, the news of this is ours to sing,
and from the tinkling bells of art's most perfect

stanzas, truth should ring, as if from the steeple
of some verbose church.

Poets must set aside rivers they never fished
to show the way to mountains we never climbed,
to paint vistas of peace and brotherhood
that could yet be, to write breadcrumbs and clues,
to help our brothers see the road to Xanadu.

Nude in Blue

A nude must be sung with a silent trill
beneath a gentle sky,
painted with the softest brush that
a verbose necromancer may conjure.
To sing her true, as curves relax
will tax the quiet strength of pen
to find her alone, in a moment
of mergence with light of moon,
or languorous in the arms of sun.
She wears adjectives with grace
but nouns must take care to whisper
like the breeze that touches her
with that most subtle ardor,
in the absence of intrusive verb.

Now, she stretches near the blue
in a frozen moment where the
sand oozes under the verge
of an inland sea, supine, at the edge
of the world, a painting, seen only
by the moon and a poet.

Rebirth

As parchment wrinkles
and yellows beneath the pen
of years

it is the pure of clouds
that gleam

I yearn for a wordless world
to fill again
with phrases, kind and
sure

on a vast and empty field
of white

Thanksgiving 2010

What blink of moon's great eye
inspires poesy of thanks?
What moist sylph of muse?
Perhaps, just the sibilant sigh
of mother night,
muttering forgiveness…

Woman

Woman is that elegant design
that carries us to earth
and blooms for none
but love.

Responsibility

 A wordslinger wears
   a harness of verses
   into the church
   of the collective mind
   into the future
I will carry mine up
   the courthouse stairs
   up to the microphone
   at the open-mic
   into the airwaves
   into the library
I will not forsake this load
   but weigh it down
   with verse to curse war
   to raise our eyes
   to sun
   to pry the hands
   of commerce
   from poetry's throat
   with placards
   that illuminate monsters
   and dim warlords
I will not forsake language
   with the excess masturbation
   of poems about nothing
   much like Billy
   but write loud
   carve a thunderous
   yawp

   lest someone has ear
   for something

Submission

It's hard to let them see you
when you don't hide in daffodils.

If they sneer through academic eyes
at entrails, displayed like lace
in stanzas of nudity
writhing like lost
lovers or other
pain ~
vulnerable
when your sacred song is found

wanting
and your verbose children romp
in a circular graveyard
while Billy doesn't fish
the Susquehanna a million times
and Walt slumbers ~

forgotten
it gets harder
to submit

but the eyes of the future
need nourishment
beyond the politics
of university politics
and self-aggrandizing scraps
of nothing much

so we write organic poems
with breasts, moans, orgasms,
and grievous wounds,
hope, and jubilant rain,
wound 'round the language
William blessed, we

 submit,

and hope for the best.

Millennium, Notes from America

While the fists of Zion pummel red crosses
and Charlie the tuna weeps
the sheep keep bleating of peace.
The electronic highway is congested
with the zeitgeist of warbling sparrows
shooting arrows of discontent over the bows
of the citizen ships.
Oh, proud vampires, extracting interest from stones,
leave the peasants alone in your great thirst.
Your coffers are more readily filled
with the lucre of kings.
Oh farms, oh, hopeful parents, you send your sons
to make amends of blood for wrongs
better left in jerky newsreels; you kneel
before diseased leaders who demand your pound of flesh
in return for freedom songs, sung by false musicians.
Your sons are not born for munitions, but for the plow,
the grain drill, not the oil drill, a bitter pill to swallow
for a patriot, but listen - the trumpet's blare rings hollow.
When the leaders are false as the profits,
you mustn't follow.

A bitch-wolf howls from the North, and leaping lemmings follow.
Her tone is violent, her invective, hollow
but hungry ears swallow her spittle like wine, and dine
on the thin soup of her anger, and this voice from the short bus
rings like thunder across the land of corn and beans.
Everything is not what it seems.

POETS, oh lost voices of the golden age, repent
the scourge of empty verse to rise against the dragons,
raise your pens again to defeat the dogs of war,
HOWL peaceful adjectives into the very maw
of war's vast wind to sing the songs of love.

Oh wind, forgive the bloated businessman, spewing his soot

into the breath of god to carry his Viagra- bloated power
to distant lands, when he lands, he is just a weak, pink,
round man, who exercises his false power over
the genitals of women who sell the moon to
a virus that spews his jizz on the face of cursed daughters.
He is only what we allow him to be.

Forsake the angry bark of the fox, who always lusts for blood,
to listen to the voice of the dove.
Anger has no place in our garden, which grows
when tended with love.
History is replete with wars, with mistakes we mustn't repeat.
Strangers are not to be defeated, but befriended,
the meek, to be defended, not conscripted
to meet the monster's ends, but embraced
as brothers.

If these new friends love other gods, relax,
there is room beneath the sun
for everyone.

Don't be beguiled by tyrants and kings
that are better reviled, just treat
your fellows as you treat
your child.

Ode

I love you
now
but you leave me
a million times
a day

The Damp Napkin Poems
        Birth

This is not my large automobile.
This is not my beautiful wife.
This is not my warm Placenta.

Catching Frogs

The first time I saw a creek
I immersed myself in lazy water
and followed it to the god
that oozed between my toes.

Awake

Jesus left me behind
on his way to Viet Nam
but I couldn't be a poet
because Peoria was so
not Patterson,
but the barges took me to Cairo
and the very banks
of extremity – home
and the only buffalos
counter-balanced nickel bags
while drums thrummed
like menstrual tides
from the skins of mystic
aboriginals in the first nations
to welcome me to iron towers
and the juggernaut of marching
dollars at the end of feeling.
I named me fox or trickster
and the joke was on the citizens
and white 1968 Ford Country Sedan
was a poor address to mail shit to
but a fine home for itching feet
that marched on the path to
Pandemonium, because, after-all
it lies at the gate from Peoria
to Patterson, or perhaps
to Xanadu.

The Skipped-Pill Marriage

 led to a sorrow dumpster, and rage
that rode me like four horses,
but the white one won the race
and I flailed oatmeal arms
and screamed propaganda
at the suits that so arrested me
on the path to my own barbaric yawp
that echoed over the roofs of
kings and such dim fables
of heroism that my god moved
six thousand miles eastward.
But it was time for leather and mayhem,
for ribald expeditions to the
slippery road home, and my
v-twin voice broke the night
and lubricated the dreams
of women who yearned
for a ride to Patterson.
Lao Tzu was so Machiavellian,
so militaristic, and Jesus so war-like that
the patch on my back read
independent.

Chaos

Death would have none of me then
as if I would poison the very ground.
Around every corner, there were monsters
that filled me with excuses
to build abattoirs and walls,
to redefine excess as success
and wax eloquent with a demon's mouth
and dare any god to risk my ire
as my tires ate America like
teeth of fire, and the grease of innocents
fertilized my beard.
I was Josho's dog, disqualified
from the quest for the Buddha spirit
as surely, as military, as Lao Tzu.

River

The first time I floated
on a river, on an inner tube,
on a butt-load of clean acid,
and watched the northern lights,
I stopped struggling on the edge
of the great divide.
I felt the star-carbon flow
in what remained of my veins.
I knew that Patterson was everywhere.
It was fitting that I was found
by a river girl with hair like Illinois
corn silk, and no fear of a pirate
of my ilk, but filled with tender mercy
for a wretch in search of nothing,
for such a feral electron.

America

I heard indigenous circles fill the air
with sand paintings, pierced my flesh
like a dim caricature of a sun dancer,
found myself a brother of all,
found myself in the farmer's callous,
the birth scream of mothers,
the tug of moon and fire, of sun;
found myself in thunder and song.
I found myself in overalls and
tie-dyes, dancing with muddy feet in the rain,
found myself in Mississippi tears,
dripping from dobro strings and
knife-fights, in the collection plates
of bloody churches that forgot
that Jesus was a hippy too,
found myself in the register of deeds
where they said I owned the earth that owned me,
found myself in the ranks of the
treasure trove of maize, the maze
of maps and rivers of a land so blessed
that it fed the very planet, tapping my heels
together in the hope that some president
would see the very beauty of America
and let those sacred mothers keep their boys.

Love

That love infect the blackest sheep
and so renew his spirit's light
that into ink the sun may creep
was proof against my endless night.

By she, who brought that light to bear,
by river's song, and lover's arms,
I left the realm of Baudelaire
to craft for her a tiny farm.

My redemption sprouted from seeds
I planted where the river sings,
and mother sun made night recede,
as if winter gave in to spring.

By light of moon, I found my way
to a garden where children play.

□

Procreation

From the ins and outs of the dance,
and the revelry of a jubilant gardener,
another seed was sewn in sacred soil
and Fauna populated my microcosm
as if my unnamed god anointed my search
for Foxfire glee with the light
of certain magic, with evidence of drums,
and bade me fill the void in me
with tendrils of flute-song, where once
sex pistols dueled in a mind cluttered
with certainty.

Silence

I found my voice in my choices
and in the lee of violence.
Love renounced the dragons
of war and the merchants
that drank my sweat like
distant vampires, renounced
the rocket's red glare, and
the dripping teeth of those
who made of Jesus an excuse
to prey on their fellows,
but Ronnie's minions made her
watch them prod my face with guns,
made her watch them silence me
lest my proclamations of peace
spread to other citizens,
lest my seeds of thought
germinate in the soil of a
soldier's mind, lest I illuminate
unwelcome truth, and I disappeared
into the garden for decades.

It was good enough for Abby, so
it was good enough for me, this
giddy sort of obscurity, this avenue
that led me closer to nothing.
I only left my county once a year,
and I painted my very flesh
with hieroglyphics, a gaudy map
to the yellow brick road, the uniform
of the others.

Patterson

A dim bulb from Texas
lit the way to Patterson
when the future seemed to need
the very salve of poems
to gird the fruit of my loins
against the march of decay,
against the poisonous preachers
that advocated suicide in the name
of prophets and profit.
My yawp flew over the roofs
of palaces, banks, battlefields,
infected the airways through the portal
opened by first nation radio,
and the hydraulics of the river
propelled these spears of word
through the wind of four
directions; clumsy missives
carried the secrets of nothing
to minds cluttered with the white
noise of the virus of knowledge,
the anthems of the damned,
the "No Fat Chicks" bumper sticker
on a big-ass pickup, bound for hell.
I wrote new anthems with the
subliminal peal of a long-forgotten
bell hanging cracked, but unbroken.
I painted word pictures of the circles
the first nations saw, sculpted
a tiny diorama of paradise at the end
of a long road that kept everyone
but the riff-raff out, the flotsam and jetsom
of a world gone mad; invited the reader
to come dance to new anthems,
whispered to northwind in the lexicon
of a wooden flute, whispered to the future
with vast and illegal breath.
Never mind the critics, fuck 'em if they
can't take a joke.

Failure

When the lies are available
at Wal Mart for $9.95, and the truth
makes hope as dear as diamonds,
the lipsticked pig prevails,
and they call Billy Collins a poet
on public radio with tiny plastic flags
waving in a sooty breeze – alas…

The seemingly never ending death of a poet

Tired, disillusioned, I embraced
the diagnosis like a balm,
like a new sort of womb, a well earned
tomb where fools and unread poets rest,
but, stubborn to a fault, unresolved
to lay my words in some lead- lined
vault where unread poets rest,
I answer each new test, bruising
my chest to take one more breath,
to squeeze out one more stanza of unrest
in a world gone mad, to attest to the
fact that my tribe is chasing doom.

It is not moot that I struggle so,
that I spend my extra days at play
in a field of words, that I howl to the deaf
that one day we mend the fence
between homo sapiens and our one
dear mother, that the voice of the others
is heard beneath the chatter of commerce
and shame to show the way to Xanadu, to Patterson,
to peace, to show the folks with the most
how to love those with the least,
to incite one soldier to plug his gun
with a flower, to infect the heart of man with hope,
lest Fauna perish beneath a mushroom cloud
for Jesus or some large map to hell.
I want so to rest, beneath my garden's soil,
but, every day boys die for oil -
my test has not been met,
so I guess the garden ain't
ready for me yet.

Star Stuff

Carl said we were all star-stuff,
but I was too high to see it.
When Moby told me the same,
I named myself Orion, named me
forever that had lived for eons,
and would, like a feral nimbus
surrounding incantations from
an invisible mouth - a very sun.

My wee poems are carbon-based;
navel gazing creatures that see
galaxies inside me, in the great we
of circles beyond the comprehension
of those trapped in but five clumsy
senses, oblivious to the consequences
of building false stars to drop
on our fellows, to char those others.

I only have this disguise because
the great mystery wanted to reward my
searchlight with the giddy friction,
the sacred throes of love, to let me
dance to the divine clock of moontide.
Oh great divide, oh ego that sponsors
factions who name the mystery
and inflict deceleration on other electrons;

why must you strive to devolve us all
to the carbon whence we came?

If II

If ambition wore mercy's face
hunger would feed beyond
borders and maps to love abound.

If circumstance looked askance
at war and saw rainbows
around the root of peace

could time be counted softly
with plenty for the least
beyond divisions
on a world
so round

as this.

Dancing With Myself

I see anger in mirrors
    one-way that hardens glass
against intruders
  with compelling arguements ~
a malignant growl

claws reach for soft
  purchase not bought
        not sought with poems
or caught in lucre's
            gilded trap

now I'm dancing
        with myself.

Theoretically, Highway Sixty-Three

I'd heard the voices since sixty-nine,
   heard them whisper
    like some wizard with a grand design,
    a need to raise a sun-burnt thumb;
    pack a bums knapsack with hope
    and ride the summer north.
I sallied forth in patched blue jeans
    to vistas of forest so deep and green
    that Henry's ghost awoke in me
    somewhere along highway sixty three.

The girls up there had sunlight in their hair
    like tie-dyed fields of dandelions
    that bloom along a sparkling river's lair
    where dancing water sings a happy song
    and birdsong fills a cleaner air;
    while trout bite all day long.
Soldiers were marchin' off to Viet Nam
    but my wizard had a different plan;
    I was to be a peaceful man, planted
    along the banks of a river, gleeful,
    on the shore of highway sixty-three.

No need for wealth, no fortune or fame,
    just a garden in a sunny glen, a girl
    that danced naked, devoid of shame,
    a girl that would quiver, again and again,
    and abstract trout for a fisherman.

No more running like a hamster on a wheel,
    no subterfuge, no more dirty deals,
    just a land as naked as us, a river,
    a woman I could trust, a sky so full
    of stars, it makes us shiver, lights
    that seize the night above the trees
    along highway sixty-three.

I planted seeds in that hallowed ground.
    The children grew amongst the corn and
    beans, the likes of which you never seen,
    with a propensity to clown around
    like buzzing little bees around my
    yellow-haired flower in seas of green.
A hippie's life is a groovy thing, an excuse
    to dance, to sing, to eat the fruit
    our big blue mother brings with love,
    to raise our crop with kid gloves,
    go fishin' knee-deep in the river
    along highway sixty-three.

The leaders, down in Washington, try to
    fill callused hands with glory and guns,
    but, tucked away in a forest of hope
    the children of the sun forsake
    the hounds of war, the grasp of lawyers
    and other whores, to breathe free,
    to flow like the gentle river, and cope.
When I sleep, plant me under the big pine tree,
    over by the garden, where I can hear
    the crick, pet the old dogs in the shade,
    watch my yellow-haired girl continue
    the grand and simple life we made
    so many years up the river you see
    riding the length
    of highway sixty-three.

Heavy Horse

I rode the horse
until she rode me.

I climbed off
amidst sweat
and screams

riding a four-poster
that bucked like

oblivion.

God?

God is like a bartender;
we all turn to him at last call.
He is the face we see in
the mirror, ready to forgive
last night's transgression.

He's the antidote for death
in minds too small
to drink deep
of life; an excuse to feel
better than the one
who does not
know him
and kill that fellow.

When I'm dead
that is what I'll be,
and god will live on
in another weak
man's mirror.

Old Farm

I sat on the seat of the disintigrating harrow,
rusting it's way into tomorrow,
and I could see the lather on the flanks
of a long dead heavy horse.

We're used to it now, the giggling, coming
from the hay mow, the screams
of sheep from the shed,
the ghosts.

It was only fitting that we planted the seeds
of love in the soft loam of the garden,
secure in the dogma of dirty sex.

Who? Why? Who? Why? Who?
Even if I'm equipped with bourbon and patience,
a chair on the porch, it is always the Owl that has
the last word.

In the spring, I dug the hole, between the dogs
and the garden, left the soil handy for them.
I hope I don't fill it anytime soon.

The Bell with the Raspy Voice

It hangs to sing of freedom,
to sing with a voice of truth,
but the bell that we forged
for our children
is cracked.

We brandish a warrior's fist
at nations of the meek
and bury dead red men
in heavily edited libraries.

We take from the poor
to feed the rich their caviar,
nail a foreclosure notice
on the middle classes' door
while CEOs clamber
for more, more

always more

but there is hope for the
children of freedom,
tomorrows keepers of the
flame, the peace, if only
we again remember to rejoice,
to honor the song of freedom
in the sound of the bell

with the raspy voice.

Clothesline

There is a clothesline near the garden
where the softest armor flaps
in the breath of summers past.

The birds sound like temple bells
in an imagined Xanadu,
a mother's voice, singing
her one true song to a
basket of basking baby,
giggling at the morning.

There is a porch where I sit,
welcoming the sun, with coffee
and a good dog, a flask,
a three foot length of hemp
away from happy,

forty years north of the basket,
thirty-five years south
of trust,

waking the day with blues
from the old marine band
and all the shirts

are the same size.

A Thorny Sort of Armor

His mistress rides a centaur on my back.
Yin and Yang align to the left and right.
It seems my artist has a magic knack
for engraving spirit guides to the light.
Gods and demons are seen to make a pact
to map my inner path from dark to light.
Beauty blooms on flesh the needles attack,
but the "citizens" look on me with fright,
pointed reminders of our nation's lack
of acceptance for we of flesh so bright
compared to plain wrappers of white or black,
and in this magic skin lies my delight.
The multicolored tribe, adorned with art
will just have to live with leers from old farts.

Tracks

i've read the tracks
of poets
and healed the tracks
of shame

 i've wept at the sight
of tracks leading back

 marveled at the ones
leading out -

but the ones that
lead to holy places

are the tracks

I'm standing in

Random Notes

It occurred to me today that the man with no god
    falls farthest -
    but, absent crutches, rises higher.
I look at the garden that feeds me, and look forward
    to feeding it.

                    *
                    *
                    *

I ponder the plow truck, buried in the snow, and gain
    perspective.

                    *
                    *
                    *

The man with no money is poor, the one with no friends,
    destitute.

                    *
                    *
                    *

Men run the world, sans ovaries, very good at killing,
    but incapable of giving birth.
The earth is finite, but we would rather destroy the planet
    than die when we are supposed to.
We pay soldiers more than teachers, athletes more than
    presidents, dishwashers more than poets.

                    *
                    *
                    *

The earth, we are told, will abide,
but the open-eyed must wonder.
Where on earth can my children hide
from the warrior's dark thunder?

I hear the distant children cry
when the bombs tear them asunder.
I voted for change, but he lied –
innocents pay for my blunder.

I shout the truth to deafened ears
of a seemingly doomed species
while presidents prey on our fears
with self-serving verbal feces.

When will we listen to the crone
and forsake the merchant's dread moans?

*
*
*

We are, you know, all made of stars, of ample carbon circles
    and opposite me on the color-wheel,
    my brother spins, another dervish, run amok
    like me, another pest in the garden,
    that chases his tail like I chase mine.

Where then, is the hope for humankind?
The only place I can find it is in the eyes of a child,
    in the wonder.
Perhaps our answers are our sins, the killers
    of the right questions.

Bible

They slammed the bible shut on my pecker
when I was a little boy,
but it throbbed forever.
Oh, I found god allright,
found it in a sacred forest,
where the aforementioned pecker
goes in, and people come out.
Now, I go to church every night.

Yo, God!

I don't know if you noticed, but folks been killin' one-another in your
names. Now you know, and I know, that it's wrong, that in all of your
guises, be they a hippy from the desert, a re-born fat man, the sun,
moon, the earth, you show them, tell them how to behave, but they ain't
gittin' it.
The old folks and scientists are preying on their young, the rich,
feeding on the poor,the pale ones preying on the tan ones, and the men
just ain't got a clue about the magic and sacred nature of wimmin.
Dude, I live in a small American town, and I'm scairt to let my daughter
outta' the house.
We're all chasin' our tails down here, God, chasin' scraps of green paper
that don't mean a DAMN thing, really. We gotta have that big-ass TV,
that SUV, but we don't hold mercy in our hearts. Here in America, the
rich folks don't do nothing. Used to be, the rich men were captains of
industry, big farmers, timber barons, men who started factories, and
published newspapers that told the truth. Now they just sit in big
offices and trade the money they rob from the little guy back and forth.
They buy all the papers and TV news and lie to us with big ceramic
smiles, screw us with fake viagra erections, fixed elections. They say
it's all good, 'cause they go to church, hear you whisper in their ears.
I know you got a busy schedule and all, but we could really use a hand
down here. I love my grandbabies, God; I try to live right, teach the
kids to love one-another, turn the other cheek, remember the message
about the meek. I plan to git a couple doctors off the public tit, die
when I'm supposed to, but I'm just one little man, and not that great a
one, at that. I hope you can see your way clear to help us out a little.
Yer ol' pal, Rob

February Rain

It feels like an oozing misery
sliding down the back of your neck.
It roots foot to grime of slush,
the soul to the rotting leaves
of yesterdays.

There is no tomorrow
in February rain; tightened buds
acknowledge no future
and even the gracious hips
of woman seem clenched.

The color is gone. This
monochromatic graveyard accepts
our measure of death
as tears, from a
tired sky.

The Rotten Egg Polka

The golden goose is dead.
We strangled it
with the noose of war.

Boogie Down at the Brokedown / Cocktails in Surrealia

There were bikers, guerilla gardeners,
pirates, to inflame blonds, dancing in
low self-esteem corner; all tube tops
and erect nipples; already lubricated.

The lesbians were shooting pool with
the post-game softball jocks, while
an albino bluesman gutted the night,
a savant guitarslinger, under blacklight.

{ever seen an albino under blacklight?}

Out back, in the bus, we couldn't spell
existentialism, but we snorted it,
smoked, shot it, tossed it back like
flaming shots of momentary amuck.

Billy was getting head in the head from
sunshine while midnight saw blood
splatter gravel out back, glittering
like angry rubies in mercury vapor.

None of this is true, of course, but
the iron horse out front, the lipstick red
Harley with the apehangers, the taildraggers
and shotguns, the chrome that shined
like new money; that scooter was mine…

The Echo of Thunder

Oh man
    that has fallen deaf to the echo of thunder,
    the thrumming drums of first nations
    on the blood-trail of wounded tribes,
    to what resounding rhythm will you mend?
or bend yourself to drink from a stream, put aside
    the schemes of gather men to dream of what
    that water's made of?

When will you question the tenants of kings;
    when will you ask them why the freedom rings
    from a bell that fires projectiles of iron
    into the breasts of minstrels that sing to sun and rain,
    to the heartthrob of thunder in drums.

I sing the Aborigine, that knew that thunder well,
    that knew hell was in the minds that fail
    to wonder, to wonder as a verb to ingest
    the noun.

I sing the Aborigine, that knew that thunder well,
    that knew the path by following smoke
    to the skys, that like the thunder, spoke
    in the rhythm of the human heart.

Oh man,
    that has fouled our mother's highways so,
    that has built cannibal guns, and hunted men,
    that has blotted out the very sun with
    unholy smoke from the vast pipes,
    of industry and iron horses on concrete rivers,
    that has eaten tribes in a vampiric hunger
    for our very mother's thick clot of menses,
    the ancients, buried beneath her very skin,
    that has killed our kin for the coins on their eyes,

that has befouled the mouths of poets with empty prose,
that has turned fire-hoses on the tribes we bought,
that have fought, and fought, and fought,
for gods we found leering in our mirrors,
what never-ending horror we have wrought.

One man plays a wooden flute, to refute all this
    because a kiss is still a kiss, the dark, remiss
    in deserting the light so soon.
He swoons in harmony to the call of a mating loon,
    plays the rhythms of the moon on stretched skins
    in time to the tides of woman, croons holy tunes
    to the womb of sky that understands his wordless song.
He see's the world in disarray, but also children, at play
    'round the maypole, their laughter, curing the sky
    and he lets this fecund song anoint his brain.
The screams of many Hiroshimas echo in his mind's eye
    like a sty with tangled roots, and streams of blood resound
    from ancient mounds in flat Illinois that remind him
    of the drums in Red Cliff, the drums in Africa,
    the circle drummed hippies in enlightened deadlots,
    alive with the simple awe of simple tribes,
    with flutes, with drums and didgeridoos, with skins
    on wooden frames, and feet that keep time
    with those tides of ancient blood, and again,
    he hears the thunder, and swells with hope,

"counting coup no more forever"

But then, he watches the evening news, sees them in the pews,
    fired up at the prospect of killing other men with other gods,
    sees them picking through the rubble of bombed-out schools,
    sees the poisons we spew into the breath of nameless god,
    sees the tribes reduced to tourist attractions for merchants
    under the golden arches of a plastic world, and sighs...

Oh man

Barefoot

Our children grow strong
that romp barefoot
in the garden that does not bow
to urban myths of shame
to preachers of plastic
servility
or the corsets
of cotton that pricks
the skin of slaves

Our get will adorn themselves with
sap, with the ministrations
of love that knows no fear
of remote reprisals

They wax organic in the
sunlit hive of youth
wrapped in the poetry
of mother's verses
and gentler winds
that will not be shackled
by polyester judgement
that hides behind black robes
of carrion crows
that acknowledge but one path
to gods that deny the touch of
flowers, of earth's warm breath

These daughters of earth
will not stand behind our sons
but lead them from the vegetables
to the clarion-call of
trumpet vine that carries flowers
into the breath of god
to the stars
that we are all
crafted from

Our sons will greet them as
frames for pictures
of immortality
and the grail of men
deemed worthy of
grace that may not
be claimed but earned
in the pantry of dreams

The seeds that carry us
into the soil of tomorrow
will be spirit-clothed
bound to the loam that feeds them
by callused feet
dancing to birdsong and love
their own singular song
barefoot
from head to toe

The red-headed step-child, and other myths

Warm is the allure of a red-haired lass
with freckled catfish skin so soft,
and those eyes that twinkle like azure glass,
their hair - spun fire, reaching aloft.
Carrot-top lads dare dream to reach higher,
as if spirit raise them high above
those drab hued boys that so raise their ire
with their misconceptions of love.
See, those lithe and gentle folk, topped with flame,
are grist for creation's vast wheel,
the singers, the painters, who make their names
of stronger stuff than mere steel.
Toast the red-headed comrade or lover,
with new realms of warmth to discover...

raise your glass to the red-haired lass.

REBUKE!

When he/she of ill
temper, low self-esteem
should refute the sun in you,

REBUKE!

When kings of men
shed blood again, and
again,

REBUKE!

When the voices of earth
are lacking mirth; all
thunder and mayhem; all
chaos and ash,

REBUKE!

When your mirror will not
divulge your beauty
to dark and hollow
eyes,

REBUKE!

If silence overtakes your song,
if all the arrows are pointed wrong,
and no one sings along,
when the stream of life flows wrong,
just curse the very night,
with verses, strong and right -
let your little light shine,
on darkest shadow,
and let your voice

be heard,

REBUKE!

Motherfucker

It was his mother, really
that taught him to take what can only be given
and driven by her surrender
to the iron will of a weak man
capitulation came to smell like love
and the weak boy curled a man's fist
His mother, really
that taught him that a woman's loving arms
must be pinned to the grimace of lust
and harm be subverted to pleasure
So trust, that greatest gift
remain untasted in his kitchen of fear
He hears their cries as sweet nothings
whispered into the ear of the spear wielder,
The great weight of the moment that sublimates joy
for ever and ever in that spasm of woe
reverberates as recompense, as pain he owes
for the fear of daddy's disrepute
He cannot refute the only law he knows, the
law of fist and claw, the graceful arch of neck
never kissed, but grasped like a fool's money,
like a flower crushed in a bankbook,
while recessed in some forgotten nook of racial memory,
he yearns for tender mercies
It was his mother, you see
that taught sissy to wear the sunglasses of love,
that taught her that a sorry fixes everything,
that mixed in with the prescription of bliss,
a man is remiss to leave out violence
So sissy died for love
and Sonny curled his fists
within a mist of fables of
angry Casanovas

It was his mother, you see,
that bore her bruises like valentines,
that signed her own, Love, Hannah,
to choose those bruises over tender fealty
to some unknown suitor that knows
that a caress is best to ignite
the love that Sonny never witnessed
So Sonny strips the daughters of the moon,
and in jejune pursuit of love
denies the bloom of many daughters,
the shine of any suns, to be forever
the rain that drowned grace,
mother's little monster

and it is mother's face he sees
every time another mother's daughter
loses the sun

Garden

Gauzy pets guard this niche beneath wooden ramparts
bearing inscriptions like, good boy, blessed rabbit, love.
The sun caresses clouds that form cotton islands in the
stream of consciousness that carries the ministrations
of mother raven, the hum of tiny wings, the whimsy
of a million dead poets - sibilant in the breath of
everything.

Forty by seventy feet, this oasis, and oh, the pink feet
that have grounded pixies, dancers, lovers, that have
tilled wonder as deep as the magenta of cornflowers,
as deep as the psychic imprint of knees and haunches,
the biological impact of Olympic swimmers, seeking
sweet germination, the way to the seed the moon
dropped.

Oh, sweet maize, twining with sunflowers in thrall
of each sunset to grace the face of the only place
where I feel real: oh language, that fails to paint for you
the ooohs, the ahhhs, the spinach, at the eastern
verge of my wee kingdom, the dew that so graces
the emerald field that diamonds glitter as morning
kisses the aging face that I see in the mirror of each
tiny droplet.

As seasons spin like months, and months like years,
it is here where I make my leafy bed. My eulogy
will be spelled by vines, heavy with beans, tied
to the pine to the south, reaching high, to pry at
a secret name for some deity that sent the sun to
warm us, the rain to lubricate the vast magic
circle.

Oh the circle, painted with sand by red brothers,
spun in dreidels, written in single brush-strokes,
formed by dancers, drummers, penitents, by poets,
philosophers, show yourself to the stilted man
that draws a straight line from birth to a god that
looks like him. Show yourself as each green citizen
springs from rain, to reach for the sun, to merge with
another in a miracle, to scatter seed and die, to lie
in state for the moons of mourning, and live again
as spring greets sons and daughters.

In the distance, the trucks and silver birds of commerce
try to ply the sky with paper leaves, but photosynthesis
is denied the false constructs of greed, the
hobnail boots and wingtips that insulate gather-
men from the very earth of their birth, and better
they spend a day barefoot in the garden than to
pray with jingling coins to a mirror image in mind's eye,
to a ghost that eats sin like vegetables. The circle
spins in one direction, and seeds of sin
germinate.

My ashes will feed this place, this verdant square,
and I don't need a preacher to show me the way back
 to the garden I never left.

Hey, Mister

Hey mister President, with yer promises of change,
how come you put criminals at the reins?
How many brown men will you slay
when the golden rule is spelled out so plain
in the book you use to explain yer agenda?
Again an' again, I heard you preach peace
an' the sheep still bleed in the middle east.

Hey man, we all voted for you, the hippies,
the smart ones, the black ones, the brown ones,
the Christians, the Muslims, an' even the Jews,
so how come I hear on the evenin' news
that that yer stealing from the many
to feed the few, an' pourin' all the money
into rich man's pockets; writin' us the IOUs?

Hey, Mr. Wall Street, with all yer fake cash,
America is bleedin into yer overflowin' pockets.
It's time to let the little fella' share your stash,
to limit the diamonds your concubine flashes,
and take up your place on a high court docket.
We've had enough of bein' trickled down upon
an' spendin' our money on oil seekin' rockets.

Hey Mr. judge, with all yer Viagra and shame,
take a look in the mirror; we're onto yer game.
You sit on the bench, all dressed in black,
lookin' down yer gin swollen nose
at the child in the ghetto who serves the crack,
the humble musician, who burns some herb,
don't prohibit us, or we'll prohibit you.

The jails are filled with dealers, with users;
all sent there by wealthy alcoholic losers
that never got a job 'till they were thirty-two
'cause daddy was rich so they stayed in school.
Don't jail our millions for smokin' a little boo
'till yer ready to outlaw yer Viagra an' booze;
don't mess with my daughter's right to choose.

Hey, Mr. banker, with all yer Hummers an' jets,
change is a'brewin' an' you ain't got it yet.
You rob from the poor to feed the rich,
an' expect the poor to cover all yer losses.
This time around, we're gonna let you fail,
'cause you drove the economy into the ditch,
an' some of you leeches are goin' to jail.

Hey, Mr. General Motors, with all yer giant trucks,
the world it is a'turnin', the dinosaurs, burnin';
the sky's turnin' gray, and you don't give a fuck.
Hey, Mr. coal-man, with yer black lung disease,
yer killin' us all while the earth keeps turnin'
in a cloud of yer dark excess. We're almost outta
luck, an' it keeps getting' hotter 'cause we don't learn.

Hey, Mr. Citizen, with all those voting rights,
It's time to take up the gauntlet an' fight,
resist that urge to let the status quo remain,
refuse to go quietly into a sooty black night,
and herd the monsters out of high places,
get back into our mother's good graces,
an' bring our America back into the light

before it's too damn late.

Escape From The Box

We, the ticky-tacky, exist
in a flickering
entrancer screen, full of death, full
of feminine hygene products, packed
in styrene cups
and scented adds in
the glossies at the magazine box

We, of cubicles, revolt
not at the corners
or resist with curvaceous
revolutions
but carve six-sided
self-portraits
of monochromatic package
silent

I sing the curved guerilla
with his round red rubber nose
trying to write his way round
in an angular arena
where the squares
have all the

teeth

Viagra Poem

THEY take Viagra
so they can, well into the age
of burning dinosaurs,
fuck us all.

THEY sit on benches, drunk,
and send the poor to jail
for smoking an herb.

THEY preach capitalism
on the way up
and stretch out a socialist hand,
palm-up,
on the way down.

THEY trade-in tired wives
for young pros who know
the blue pills were
really
made for them.

{movin' on up}

It's hard to enslave a people
but they are always hard now -
soft little pink men,
with hard little
peckers.

THEY giggle at the poor
Republican
that votes them all their pills,
while getting hummers
in foreign limos
with foreign drivers
while red-neck Joe can't
pay his bills.

Let's hear it for Viagra,
for the doctors
that keep them going.
THEY will live forever
to poke those little girls
and spew their wealth on a few
just to watch it
trickle down.

It's a bitter pill

to swallow.

Bourbon 'n' Blow II

We all know that blow is the key
   to the women's bathroom
   that does not smell like urine
   but a kaleidoscope of scented
   products, of mystery's folds.
In a blues bar, patrons live up to the
   lyrics, fertile ground for a poet
   with shiny shoes, and bourbon
   is the lubricant of choice.

I showed that bitch the best ten
   seconds of her life!

If Petals Fall

If you paint the depths
of me in ice,
and winter seize my eye

 should the song of us
flee into a memory

 deep in the pond
of yesterday

 I will see your softest sigh
on the face of spring's
first lotus

 as my spirit remembers
how to fly.

War Dogs

The dogs of war howl
under a smoking sky.
Victory is a liar
when youth lies dying.

It is not moot to query heroes…

Weight

The butcher has his thumb on the scales of justice,
    and we, the meek meat bleed for maps
    that envelop the serfs in rings of fire.
The banker weighs souls by the current price of gold
    that does not shine in the ghetto, in the
    tenement, in the eyes of yesterday's hero,
    twitching in the home marked Frigidaire,
    beneath the Beemers, streaming by on the way
    to Xanadu, streaming electronic sermons
    of greed and consumtion.
The kings need the unemployed, you see, to be
    all that they can bleed for leaders who use Gods
    and slogans to feather their nests with the best
    of the poor sons, to put them to wicked tests
    in the wars of diseased minds, mercenaries
    in the overlords regimes.
The first nations wither beneath the weight of plastic
    Francewater bottles and the hopeless thunderbird
    that hovers over rivers of mud and poisons,
    over casinos and plastic beads, over a dying land
    where the weight of politicians is felt in the crush
    of vice and poverty they bestow in the name
    of their neon Babylon.
The mothers of poverty are weighed down by bodies
    of sons who died for the wealthy ones, the
    captains of a mother-ship they scuttled
    to reap the harvest of salvage from the bones
    of America.

The butcher has his thumb on the scales of justice,
    his ass, on a seat between the arms of a soot –
    belching dragon, so his very feet may tear
    the skin of every land, that his steel proboscis
    may pierce each of god's four breaths
    to bleed the earth of oil, to spoil the soil,
    the air, the very sky with toxic effluent
    of ambition, our heaviest disease.

The tax man knocks on the door of the poor
   while the rich bask in the bath of excess,
   and success is measured in the false dollars
   that are so surely knitted into chains
   to bind the farmer, the craftsman, the
   builder of real things to feed them, house them,
   to ring the necks of their whores
   with diamonds.
The princes, the generals and other scavengers
   feed on the carcass of America, bleed
   the nation of its wealth, and the preachers
   plead for the proud patriot to bleed
   for the lucre of other gods, the breath of
   scattered winds, that do not know the names
   of the constructs they found in mirrors,
   and the sons of poverty bleed for these
   black- robed vultures, and the kings they serve.
The very world wobbles with the accumulation
   of wealth, the concrete monoliths of Mexico City,
   of New York, of Washington and other toxic
   waste sites where greed stamps feet of stone
   and steel, stamps golden seals of approval
   on the lead corset of the people who march
   to the tunes of cracked bells, warbling
   politicians, bellowing bankers, hungry preachers,
   Paris Hilton, and all the other evil clowns

   until we all fall down.

\   **Smell**

I am musk and incense, nectar
and putrefaction.
I am the sponsor of probing
erection and dry heaving,
of half-asleep stumbling
at the beck of brewing coffee,
of delvings into slippery caves.
I'm the author of a million
obtuse flower poems
and the breath of the world.

Only a Poet

I'm only a poet that refuses to paint rivers
I never fished or pabulum from the teat of
the fox that gnaws at the mind of America
with the blunt teeth of Dick and Jane.

I will sing from Rockland, from Naropa, from
Patterson and Xanadu, spew the diatribe
of peaceful tribes, that tomorrow's child
will know that flowers are painted with

words that fail the dim academic –
because poems are best left to heroes.

Sparkle

"The Frost performs its secret ministry," said Sam,
and, as if the breath of god were a brush,
the window glints with feathered etchings of
first ice, dancing across the face of night.

My midnight muse tickles the eye
that spies the stars through the frame
of such geometric bliss as this
subliminal hiss of silver secrets.

Eulogy

(With apologies to Maynard)

Only through me, you said
and you lied,
you lied
You disapproved so damned loud
So proud, so
damned proud
that you could chew my sins like glass
so proud
that Xanadu could only come to pass
through you,
through you

So many wars are fought for you, for
you
So many bodies broken here
for you
So many priests on altar boys
So many bleeding human toys
So many daughters soiled by men
So many fail to obey them
So many broken in in your wars
For the john of ancient whores
For you
For you

You preach of things we must not do
So many ways to miss our cue
and sacrifice the grace that grew
from a carnival of lies
with chains of lies

So many crosses carried now
in abject human sacrifice
so many heeded your advice
so many damned by your device
forgiven every heinous vice

with conscience dimmed, they roll the dice
denying mother's magic womb
to be born twice
like you

Before the lowly maggots feed
on what your father left of me
I'll stand tall on my own two feet
and count on my own scattered seeds
to speak for me
to speak for me

I'll answer for my evil deeds
without your name upon my lips
without your lies to protect me
from my fate

I'll hold my children to my breast
and to the truth, I will attest
that love's the only god they need
that love is meek man's only creed
that preachers are maggots
that feed on greedy souls

Once was I born, and once, I'll die
free of all your oily lies
and all my sins will follow me
All my tribe will sing for me
an honest lilting eulogy
when I am finally free
of you
of you

Frost and Samuel Coleridge

The first seems no curse
but the second snow is worse

His verses echo frost
that etches such diagrams
on laced eyes that the world
is frozen in stasis

When windows wax eloquent
with blooming flowers
that grip the heart like
frigid fingers
stanzas dance in rictus

Malignant lines form moans
in beds where fair inertia
sleeps for three tinged moons
that Coleridge loved so well

If I Were

IF I were a poem,
I would invite my ghosts
and lovers, my mentors and muse,
my penitentiary and tomb,
and parade them as wisps of song.

If I were a poet,
I would craft a tribe of bohemians
to paint a tapestry of days in such frosted
eyes that life would seem a lace of spun stars,
and my scars would mark a map to grace.

If I were a tree,
my arms would shelter sparrows,
and the dew would glisten on leaves
that paint the sky like sunset hair
that falls to blue tumors of winter
while I reach for songs sung by stars.
 If I were a word, I would be
complicated.

Remember the Drums

Woe is to the poet who inscribes
the ranch-style desert
in a nation of skin and bark homes –
a constabulary of rivers –
who pushes the elixir of polyvinylchloride
to citizens of iron blood

The bellowing multitude of buffalo
is silenced by the sheep
who follow the fox
to slaughterhouse five –
to the bottom line
in a museum of broken
circles

The moon still pulls at arteries
with the artistry of menses – tides -
the vast clock of universal
biology

but the empty pages of false troubadours
stand in square rows to deny
rhythm of lines
that never end

The minstrels of academic money
have forgotten to bleed –
have forgotten the drums
that call them home

Woe to the reader
of blank pages

I

am not the man in the mirror, that blind eye,
but the shimmering visage
in deep chill waters

am not my purse of dreams,
but the unseen hero of stories
yet to come

am not a purveyor of machines
or recompense, but merely a sculptor
of a verbose breast

am just a bag of meat
that bleeds in a nation
of bullets

am only a reflection of love
in volumes of fables
to read when that blue-eyed moon
blinks

Late Autumn

When the last leaf
flies from my quill
and the end is spelt
in fire

the wind will moan
with my children's voices
and the moon will echo
with stanzas of oak

Holiday

The dead sheep are quiet
in the shed, banshees
beaten back with a seventy-
nine cent bic
Snowflakes lick at geometrically
crusted eyes, and I understand
Coleridge

A storm marches across the radar
like a great tumor
seeking a sunset, but she
rides south

Baudelaire knew this season
like a slap
or a stain on a lover's brain
knew the copper menses
of the darkest
concubine
knew the overwhelming silence
of dead sheep
in november

The Very Breath of God

The wind whispers secrets
like a god devoid
of agenda,

like the truth.

The Spoon River Revisited

Down by the river, where the epitaphs
float by, by the sandbar, below the catfish hole
is a trestle, where souls scream at night
Don't matter if you have nappy hair
or ol' John Barleycorn is houndin' you
don't matter if your ol' man beat you
or your woman done you wrong
the river knows the right song for
everyone

Up on the bank, a cemetery guards the hills
with the blinded eyes of saints and sinners
ministers and thieves, monsters and mothers
and they all have their roots
in the river

You can hear 'em at night, you see,
these warbling souls, speaking in the tongue
of water over stone, oozing down that
turnpike to the sea

but me,   I'll settle fer catfish

Changes

On the cusp of nevermore
when all the leaves have fallen
it is not moot to ponder
the blue abyss

The Softest Warrior

I fight for peace with ramshackle words
that fly true like cedar shafts from a handmade bow –
cleaving the breath of god
with a sibilant hiss.

I fight for a woman god, a moon that will not
rise over battlefields or wax ironic
over notions like holy war –
a mother of bloodless tides.

I make my meat with love
and thank the stag
for my children.

I am fierce against my very enemy –

War.

Notes on waiting

and the world does not escape
the perpetual spin
for your stasis – the dock
will not flee your
stationary vessel

Tomorrow will run like sand
if you don't meet it
in the moment

that just became
a memory...

Notes from the New Right

Oh, the new friction,
like frottage at the new tea-party,
like a magnet, alienating its shadow.
Oh, the right wing of the eagle,
tearing at the wind.

The wind –
the wind, torn by the sharp-toothed fox
still lifts the flower's voice.

Fellate the horn of plenty,
gain your master's hot green spunk.
It is not our place to question the corporation.
Glorious bank,
draw me into hungry arms –
protect me from the mad socialist
with his page of propaganda.
The ghettoes would suckle, greedy, at your vast and turgid nipple
but we are here for you.

Shed the burden of the tax man,
lest the progressives infiltrate from the coasts.
We proud tea-baggers recreate beneath a bag of coins,
and never wince at the banker's sweat or groans.
Let hungry children lie
where other gods thrive –
we need our corn to power Cadillacs.
Pull out at the last moment and let your seeds trickle down
on the lower class.

Oh, diametric clash,
incite our horde to rise –
erect again our cross-tipped steeples into air
that wears the stain of industry,
anoint the breath of earth with business scents.

Poor men wait in shadows
to sup at the feet of kings,

and when they grovel,
you hear the very bells of freedom ring.
Raise your glass high to salute our proud warriors,
who bleed for god, country, and the corporate titans –
who stand tall at the head of the line.

We must suffer the rainbow cast a vote
to let them play at freedom,
while we bend them to our will
and wipe ourselves on their drapes.

Metamorphosis 54

Oh freedom, oh sweet devolution, when one is shorn –
absolved of the dim and ponderous weight of future
by a doctor, a judge, a shaman, an odd sort of mushroom
or some other circular elixir, and POP! the moment is yours.

Oh now, oh lovely primal now, in your sun-dress and nipples,
sing with me, SING as I am freed of tomorrows chains –
dance like this gibbering dervish that finally knows now,
that holds nothing like a diamond.

Oh tinkling finger-cymbals of wind, sweet salt tears of joy
that celebrate this moment so free of birth or death, oh horse
in mid gallop, flying so low over infinite prairie, sing with me.

Oh lovely O, with your endless possibility, with room
for the likes of me to bloom, absolved of knowing's girth,
with room for mirth where once such facts coagulated
that questions were forsworn for tomorrow, for yesterday,
those constructs of men who would own the wind.

Oh, unencumbered me, oh, uber-me so gloriously terminal –
who could have foreseen such freedom at the hand of
tomorrow's diagnosis; who could predict that next year
was my only jailer?

Casanova's bleeding

in an alley: in an alley in the mercury-vapor
backwash of bourbon, a broad he trusted,
and, apparently – fisticuffs.

Casanova sports a hangover like the shadow
of a disease on an x-ray nobody wants to see,
"'cause, see, that picture ain't me," we say
'cause that image is too dark to be me, too
filthy to be momma's little boy.

Midnight hangs like a dirty curtain in the
whore house at the end of the universe
or another verse of blues, textured by
straight-razor scars and quantum regret.

Casanova won't die tonight though,
no, not yet, not on this misbegotten cusp,
'cause there are always more mean women,
glittering like supernovas, ready to burn
the erstwhile astronomer, the nearest
outlier on the fringe of the human condition,
the next prestidigitator of slurred spells,
the next bon vivant.

As a grimy yellow sun rises on dumpsters
and rats, scurrying on the gritty dynamo of
commerce; files of suits, marching off
to cubicles - crucibles of porcelain
receive last night's sin, and Casanova stirs
to begin again.

There are a million floozies out there
and Casanova has a lot more bleedin' to do…

Rust

The little chair rusts in
Patterson

as if a child is long
gone

and it makes the yard
empty

so it seems the alley has
won.

Halo

It's warmer now
and different fauna thrive
as if god has changed her mind,

but we, the tricksters -

survive...

Poem Poem

Sasha wants to be a girl for Christmas
an' the poet wants breath like Ginsberg,
but, man, the cancer-sticks didn't
let him down like Hunter,
an' Chinaski ain't got nuthin' on him.

He found this poem in the bottom of a Beam bottle,
while the farm boys killed Muslims fer Jews.

He writes like a church-fart, or a hooker in a weddin' dress,
a poor Republican, a rich man with a pure heart,
the god-damn poet laureate of a one man nation.

He cries when he hears "Nighthawks at the Diner"
or watches the evenin' news, 'cause ol' Tom
is a movie star now, an' the flat screen is full of
blood an' oil.

He stands at the end of the line with a nose-bleed;
Marb red danglin' - a twisted grin, like he knows
the secret punch-line to the great American joke –
wheezin'.

He mates with calamity like a zoo-monkey
with an audience of second graders,
an' here's what he wrote –

The End.

Unheard Screams

The trees were all in rows
  and I knew I am jailed
  like the forest

How unfair that
  the lightning-struck man
  never hears the thunder

Now, the gulf will NEVER squeak

On the road
organically
pedals spinning in time with the moon
I noted civilizations
of flattened fur, feathers, smears
and I measured our progress
in corpses

nearly every dog encountered
exacted their revenge
and it was good

Trucker's Lament

If, when the hours lengthen
and my midnight wheels are spinning
a hollow voice should seem to call
and you hear the shutters closing
to clothe a naked soul

just smile up at that distant ceiling
and send me out a thought
because these miles
that dim your picture
are eating me alive
and highways stretch off
into darkness that feeds
on carrion

I'm feeling locked up
in this warehouse
just waiting for a load
and the road kill
looks like family
along the gravel edge
of a million different turnpikes
but none of them
lead home

When the farmlands grow the monsters
that try to swallow me
and all the windows seem to laugh

when I see the flashers howling
that someone else has died
and even the radio is silent
it's your face that I see,
Darlene

If I couldn't see you waiting
off some exit down the road
these endless loads of plastic
would chase me straight to hell

I think I'm somewhere north of Houston
and the nightmares are chasing me
but I hear your voice singing
while your simple tasks are done
and the moon you see out the window
is shining in my cab

I just look up at it smiling
because it's the same one
and America keeps on flowing
beneath eighteen wheels
rolling home

The Whole

There's a hole in me
where Grandma used to be,
but, see, I see her sitting there
knitting in that old rockin' chair,
smiling, as if she knew a special secret.

There's a whole in me
where my Grandma used to be,
'cause, see, I see with her glittering eyes,
I really see the garden, the diamonds in the sky,
and as I see her looking down, wearing a tiara of stars,

I know that my grandma lives on in me.

The Time is Now

Allen's lost battalion has disbanded to harvest currency
    as if the price of freedom has gotten too steep.
We export democracy with shock and awe at the feet
    of a heavy handed warrior god who dodged his
    own crusade, but put the poor man's progeny into the fray
    while his stayed home to play in oilfields and Saks.
The Texan invaded with god in his ear, his ass in the rear
    and fear to preach to the fleeced sheep that he bought
    for Haliburton; and he bought them cheap.
The air is so filthy that burned angels fall from the sky like
    pamphlets that call for the surrender of hope.
Black – robed carrion crows send poor boys to prison
    for burning a little dope while a bourbon soaked
    trophy wife gets to swill their Viagra infused pride.
Babylon is burning and money bought the matches; the
    army's made of mercenaries now to brew fresh batches
    of horror for the stew that grew out of vengeance for
    six – million Jews, but you won't hear the truth on the
    evening news, but only more excuses for bombs that
    spew from the pulpits and pews of hungry ravens.

Now, the hand that holds the black man down is brown.

We carried placards for peace in the middle-east, and
    fought rifles with daisies in Chicago and Ohio.
We marched in dresses and demanded to vote, even
    if we had a uterus or darkly pigmented skin.
We fought the National Guard, even though we couldn't win.
We built a railroad underground so human livestock could not
    be found by the darkest farmers who wielded the whip
    to flay the skin from the backs of kings who arrived
    in the land of freedom, chained in the hold of the citizen ship.
Their eyes looked back to Africa, their songs went silent, their
    ears were deaf to the ringing of a patriot's broken bell.
The pretty girls fetched a hefty price in the land of the free,
    the home of the brave man who wiped out the kings
    of the plains, the daughters of the forest, with the sharp
    retort of rifle, the Armageddon of cannons.

But we were black Panthers and white panthers, guerillas
    in the theater of public opinion, warriors in the cause of peace
    in the face of disgrace at the top of a dark dominion.
We marched in Selma, in China and L.A. We stood on the steps
    of the courthouse and burned our draft cards. We fomented
    revolution in the cause of evolution in the chaos of Babylon.
We rioted in the streets when the papers wouldn't print the truth.
We pranced about in flag shirts, all unruly and uncouth.
We danced to other drummers that demanded peace, rejected
    the teachings of violent prophets, ejected a king, ended a war.
We took on the greedy few that infested the body of America,
    some of us were arrested and others fled. Another railroad
    sprung up to hide the ones who led the sheep to peaceful pastures.
Some died in Mississippi. Some died at Kent State. Our poets
    shed blood in Chicago and many shared their fate.
The poets and the painters, the dreamers and thinkers, the singers
    of the angry songs, carried the gauntlet into the fray.

We've traded our tie-dyes for Brooks Brothers suits, and our poems
    are pointless, our messages muted by old white faces
    that grace green slips that erase the good grace of words.
Oh, language, that used to arm the philosophical army of thought;
    what price is enough for the silence they bought, those
    old rich men who fill libraries with prose poems about nothing
    much to bribe the tribes that used to spill the beans?
We've finally elected a man of color, but it seems like he only
    sees green, robbing the poor to feed the richest white men
    the world has ever seen.
We already have war and he wants more. Kill a lot of brown fellas
    to even the score, get them to retaliate so we can kill some more.
He fails to understand that we read men by Braille, that a liar is tested
    by his word, not his skin, and the words we heard again, and again
    were promising changes to the structure of a nation that enslaves
    the middle-class, but none of that has come to pass, and the wealthy
    are covered in jewels that are earned by masses, straining
    against their chains in the land of the free, the home of the brave.

The best minds of a generation have been stagnant for thirty years.

The time is now to rise again from the ashes of America, to write the
  poems of discontent, to sing our songs of peace and brotherhood
  to the disintegrating wind, demand that war-mongers relent
  in their rape of our language, calling kidnapping rendition
  in the third edition of history, calling the grand inquisitor
  Uncle Sam, calling slavery trickle-down economics while
  anybody that resists colonialism is termed a terrorist.
The time is now to pick up our pens, to write unruly poems again.
The time is now to speak up for the silent girth of the very earth,
  to sing our songs of peace again to the ears of all our sheep,
  to remind our new king that he has promises to keep.
It's time again, to raise an eloquent voice in alarm at the thoughts
  of "clean coal" of "extraordinary rendition" and nuclear fission.
It's time again, to rise up in the streets, the ghettoes, the factories,
  the farms, to carve into the awareness of our children, the fact
  that without the farmer, the merchant will starve.
The time is NOW for the sheep to bleat at the wolf, to step up to
  microphones and hurl the truth like spears of love, to pierce
  the very air we breathe with epithets of rebuke for the lords
  of war and misery, words of denial of the spooks that haunt
  the halls of justice at the money lenders behest, to beat our
  chests, to answer out greatest test, and HOWL at the top
  of our lungs that the time for change is now; its
  time for the meek to claim our inheritance.

Touching God

Sometimes I hold a thing, a
flower, a sheaf of lettuce,
a breast,
a poem, a thorn,
a child's chin,

and it seems as if my hand
is becoming,
as if that butterfly or spider-web
adorning it

is part of god and

everything.

Self Portrait

(For Sal}

I've painted myself,
 screaming

with a stolen brush
that resonates like an old
national or some other
nomenclature

voids appear silently
like holes in the afghan
grandma knitted
between funerals
and amniotic fluid
between paisley and
capitalism, intestines and tired
saints

 there may be poems whispered
from prisons or orgasms
executed by stuttering colors
that clot where
unborn children play
with crones in vistas of
empty ocean in blues

 I am god because I sling paint so
profuse and profound
that these very verses
are aroused with rivers
and curses,
balm for the pages of libraries
that were aborted
years before they were built
to hover over an endless river
of words

But god has a lower case i
on a muddy palette
where crows fly, unimpeded
by traffic or shame
to carouse in the winds of change
mumbled in the silent languages
of ancient mariners
that know each eon
is an empty canvass
waiting for the color
of stories

so I sing my songs aloft
with blood from a stolen brush
on Monday

Triad

Small faces

look up from the leaves of me,
as winds of time rustle deteriorating
paper with old voices reminiscing
about ancient glories
as I rock, and write
the past to life
in rhyme, and wonder
if this is how
the world ends.

Geopolitical Reality 2009

My mother's face is cracked
where California rubs up against
America.
The banker ate the farmer
in New York City
and it all was the fault
of the sheep.

Ghost # 52

I see myself in the pond
but it's the me I used to be
and the pond is
still clean.

Given the reality of the old man,
I believe I prefer to see
my ghost.

The Great Society

Never mind the man behind the curtain
gesticulating like a broken-winged
albatross
His incantations form no remedy
for blindness
in sheep

Never mind the man behind the bullhorn
shrieking about Armageddon
in sing-song rhymes
that paint kings with disaster adjectives
and shame

Never mind the nappy-headed white man
taking tentative steps, weaving
along a good red road
as if god failed him in the latest
crusades, in the latest

judgements,
or his own realization
of god's birth
from the womb of some man's
mirror

Never mind that voice on the radio
that wavers with the hiccups
that follow invisible tears, the hallucinations
of grandchildren, burned
at the stakes of someday
with piles of green papers
providing the immolation
of innocents, never mind
the prophets who refuse
to adopt the lemming's path
but raise unruly voices
against the warlords
in Washington,
the vultures
on the carcass of America

Never mind the old man in the garden, weeping

Never mind the old man in shackles
the one that noticed that a black Bush
is yet a Bush, with thorns
for the middle class, and lobsters
for the soft pink predators,
bombs for brown men

The gulag awaits
the honest man
with open eye disease
and exaggerated
adjectives

Small faces

look up from the leaves of me,
as winds of time rustle deteriorating
paper with old voices reminiscing
about ancient glories
as I rock, and write
the past to life
in rhyme, and wonder
if this is how
the world ends.

Geopolitical Reality 2009

My mother's face is cracked
where California rubs up against
America.

The banker ate the farmer
in New York City
and it all was the fault
of the sheep.

Love Poem

I tried to write a poem for a contest
seeking love poems, but
all I could think about was my friend,
all those love letters he writes
to Squeaky Fromme,
in the form of sonnets.

I tried to write about Emily,
but I never knew her,
and plagiarism fails to lubricate
the page with spurting ink.

I tried to find a rhyme for onanism
but lost myself in the rhythm
of angels, the recompense
for an excess of friction.

I tried to write long lines,
but thoughts of big gay Allen,
my grandmother,
and cellulite interrupted
the movies in my
pen.

I tried to write from an enlightened
perspective like Bly,
with tender flesh, beneath a
northern sky,
but I could only summon love
for the skinny bitch
in the pictures with
Bukowski.

Killing Me Softly

She loved me for a while
while April danced like rain
on our first tulips,
and the early evening was
cut by the sound of
scissoring thighs.

Later, there were expectations
and the clothing of love
wore drab colors
to a missionary church
where the collection plate
was empty of sighs.

My midnight was the dull end
of a knife that cuts softly.
Armageddon had a gentle voice
that still loved me a little
in the grip of February's arms.
I was amputated quietly

with a goodbye kiss...

Touching God

Sometimes I hold a thing, a
flower, a sheaf of lettuce,
a breast,

a poem, a thorn,

a child's chin,

and it seems as if my hand
is becoming,

as if that butterfly or spider-web
adorning it

is part of god and

everything.

Revolution

When all our feet dance
    to one drum
that echoes tides
    and the sun shines
on a rainbow

the children will embrace
    one mother.

When my spirit knows
    that the wounds
I inflict on a contrasting
    brother
make me bleed
    I will be a citizen

    of earth.

Fill My Sails

When I sail my ship to darkness
and the storm clouds gather near,
you relieve the sea's grim starkness
and gird me against my fears.
It's your whispers that fill my sails
on my journey to find peace,
and when my vessel leaks, you bail.
Your love is my golden fleece.

Be my nation, the flag I fly,
as my armada sails east;
be that thunderous battle cry
against the hungry beast.
Let me take shelter in your lee,
to plead the cause of the meek.

My cannons will roar with your voice
in the tempest of the night.
The rainbow colored flag I hoist
leads us all into the light.
For you, I'll save the albatross
Coleridge left to show the way
that we must sail, despite the cost
of a new and brighter day.

Your woman's heart, the pull of tide,
lead the way to calmer shores,
provide direction for my strides
to bid them end the scourge of war.
Your distant breath is my fair breeze,
your mother love, my decree.

My Queen, for you,
I lead the way to peace.

Change?

The rainbow spawned hope
on a lopsided ball
but the gold is still fed
to the kings
while knights fall
on distant lands.

Monsters buy poison permits
and bleed the sheep
to pay for ochre clouds
and orange flowers
still bloom to the east.

The empire is growing
while the subjects starve
on the crusts left by
princes.

Hollow words reverberate
in the head of the beggar
beneath the overpass
littered with cardboard
mansions for fallen
heroes that share one question
for the master of speeches.

Brother, can you spare a dime?

Hitchhiking to Vancouver

(for Richard Brautigan and Marc Creamore)

In my mind, I'm hitch
hiking to Vancouver
There is a wise poet
with gentle eyes, and
arms for me a brother,
an island and rain
forest
because my fair mother
my nation, has 700
military bases in
130 countries
My talismans against
war have failed my
flowers that bloomed
beneath a happy yellow
face that lit
a revolution
There are 700 trout
streams between Washburn
and Vancouver, 130
communes, a split-bamboo
Orvis, strapped to
a knapsack full of
paper and pens
I think there are 700
poems between me
and death
and 130 poets in
Vancouver

The weight of prohibition
is reduced by 700%
when the border is breached
My journey is paisley and
a stormish, bruiseish, blue
It rhymes with expansion
cracks and crack whores
in Babylon
and I think there is a sonnet
finning lazily in a Montana
stream, rising to a hatch
of ideals
I wish Tom Robbins would
write me a giant thumb
or even a blue cowgirl
for an imaginary poet
in leaky waders
on a metaphysical quest
for a grail of words
In Vancouver, there are
130 people who will
like my pomes, 700
good and gentle people
to cushion my fall
from grace

I want to hitchhike to Katmandu
or Naropa Institute, just
to say I did it
I want to hitchhike forward
to a clean, peaceful
America with my progeny
My thumbs and poems
are too weak for this
Is this how the world ends
in a poem about 130 bones
strewn about on the shoulders
of tomorrow?

Still Life with Barbed Wire

I saw a storm of horses

blow across the prairie

like clear waters

running to the sea -

and I knew that

sometimes, god is

a broken fence.

Like Medusa

You hurt me like
the pink mist in Dallas
like a broken dream
awash in a crystal
palace

but I need you like
another line

You hurt me like
Baudelaire's sweet mother
like a flooded stream
choked with the tongues
of others

but I reach for you
like something sublime

You kill me like
some well aimed arrow
break my fragile bones
just to get at
the marrow

but I think of you
all the time

so I bend to you
and lose my
mind

Letter to a Poet

Marc,
There is a particular sort of foam
(Do you know it, dear brother?)
(I fear you do…)
that fills the spaces once held by words.
I let it into deer with arrows, and into me
with Hunter's dependable suicide.

I have conjured it some small numbered times
and shuddered it out with great bellowing coughs –
with curses and poems, my own sweaty, oily, midnight wars,
but it adorns my very lips today –
thick, wet, stronger, finally, than my words.

Today, I deny the merchants, remain home, still,
Try to relax against the starving screams once more.
So soft, this foam, translucent, lovely really, as if
It simply must cushion the brink, but no,
this odd foam only sharpens those muffled screams,
and all the dreams, those diseased moments of ill-fed sleep,
are oily.

I think of our loved ones, and wish the foam would leave the poets to
pursue the warlords, merchants, and clerics.
 There is a particular sort of oil.
(Do you know it, dear brother?)
(I fear you do)
that glistens on me, cloying, in the night
when I am not awake, asleep, alive, dead, but all of them and none –
straining toward some last stanza of a story
nobody wanted to read anyway, for another
breath, another day of despair, and the oil marks me like a daub
of damnation waiting for a cat's tongue of flame
to burn away the great hidden struggle, to light the way into that
Folgers can.

This heinous gaze lights my face as if it will not be marred with tar
like the gulf where the British defeated us after-all, but
fevered with the evidence that peace was never found.
 If, somehow, tomorrow appears through the foam and the oil,
I will stop looking for nothing, endeavor to remain long enough
to assemble one last stack of unread words, the biggest one yet.
It will be named "Breathless Wind" and dedicated to my brother…

Love, Rob

Bluebells in the doorway

When the bluebells peal
in the forest
as if to fade the stinging
sound of bruise
it is not moot to hope

Perhaps, darkness is but
shade
and dormant smiles
await such trumpets
to sound the softest
sigh

I wonder if they will
still sing
in freshly disturbed
soil

fed by a poet

Notes from the Doorway to Xanadu

Though my flesh bade you bloom
and rot denies you shudders
the doorway to the earth
shines bright

A silent cacophony of sighs erupts
from that first deep breath
in years that have no gravity
in timeless lands

My hands that stroked you well
becalm the clay directly
as if to sculpt peace
beneath the very earth's face

Oh, such flowers will rise from
that new frontier, such scents arise
that the breeze will sing of love
and we will writhe in our sleeps

You will dance with me yet
where lilacs tower over violet
fed by sonnets and corn-fat
fed by a poet and grace

Somehow, beneath your feet
beyond the ken of mere man
beyond now, time, and space

I'll still see the smile
on your face

Extinction

I saw a tempest
in a teacup
as if the oil-storm
drilled my eye.

It is not moot
to personalize
extinction
in such cups.

Perhaps a little
absinthe, a little
cyanide; unwilling
to see my children

at the bottom.

Notes on the absence of the toad with the Buddha Spirit.

I started dying
the day I was born
as if I would do it well.

I paddled for years,
but I went upstream,
away from the estuary
where no god could
find me.

I spent myself in
sacred flowers and
the jaws of commerce,
spent myself in convulsions
like Elvis or some irridescent
mother who came at birthing -
all screaming with pain and glee.

The Buddha toad died
in the fourth year of drought,
and the fat stone man, with
the well worn belly is of less
consequence, like me,
but I sowed more than I reaped,
and I laughed like a dervish.

If the rains ever return,
I will be the new toad.

After the Eclipse,

when the words need no
paper,
and I meet the poet
behind the light,

I'll be well armed with
this empty mind
to be the first
outside agitator in
Utopia.

Praying without a god - again

My tribe pray without a god
and daub our throats with the blood
of the animal tribes, the vegetable
tribes, the maize peoples –
the river,
and we flood the loins of our mother
with the damned blood of ancients

As we kill our mother's breath
with greed's noxious smokes,
smokes that carry doom in black voices,
our choices read last rites
to first nations

It is not moot that my last prayers
are but gasps

***

Oh garden, oh soil, you black magic,
let me redeem myself in you –
let my spirit follow
the clear river down
to the sea that we soil with oil,
accept me with our apology

Oh tree, oh mighty pine
that will not box me
against my mother's arms –

live

Oh sky that I befoul,
with coal, with grandfather dinosaur,
hear me repent, and spare my young

from me

Oh, baby, forgive me
for shitting in my nest
in my mindless quest for more

Oh river, oh sea, scrub from thee
my filth, and

live

Oh remnant, meek aborigine,
sing for us in our need;
paint the merchant a path
to the garden, sing the king
a circle of love;
sing the lost nations home
with a circle of drums
that remember one
heartbeat, one love

Oh banker, sky-pilot,
Oh king, Oh general,
Oh, soldier, lawyer, parent –
hear their song –

and when I'm gone to you –
hear me sing along

Rob Ganson
Citizen – Upper Mississippi River Drainage

What if god

the stars look so very
special through dimming
eyes
but blind fingers still
reach for breasts
and the needle yet seeks
wet north
as browncaps lurk just off
the Louisiana nightmares
that illuminate the gulf
between merchants and
legitimate humans

I can't wait to see Anne
who knew that every turn
of every key is a
tiny suicide, a
decision not to be
a way-point on the road to death
an assault on the breath
of our mother-stone
and I, the odd man out
secrete myself as hermit
as if to deny me open
eyes, my betrothal
to the abyss

Did Baudelaire stop like this
as if to let the reaper catch up?
Did Sam really mean to hang
this bird 'round my neck?
Does anyone else pray
without a god?

Is there really anybody
out there?

Oh, hi ther...

Nobler?

Religion is the only mental illness
so widespread that those who suffer not
are seen as odd.

*

They don't even know that they
tortured me too.
It is April fifteenth again, and I wonder
how many bombs I bought god
last year

*

My lines, my breath, are so short –
but that's cool, 'cause I only want to scream
"NO!"

*

The first fool who looked
into a clear pool invented god
and killed someone for him.

I'm so glad I'm nearly done
being human.

Rage, my ass; bring it on.

Looking for Yellow

I try to paint with words and I am colored
I am but, have only I, and eye
and we see with both inner and outer
that the sky is plied with color
Navel-gazing painters like this melded me
of I, of eye and sky, paint unapologetic volcanoes
and yellow is the adjective the academics deny
The daffodil is not a color, a momentary diversion,
but a moment, promised to deny suicide
with the hue that is but an unfulfilled
promise
that

we

dance

like

gods

I revel in the pretence of dove's breast
when my test is failed on cities; all the colors melded
to find the very false balance of gray
In the storm, the sewer at the back of I mind;
in the slush of compromise and shame,
there are not but seven sorrows, but symphonies,
populations, and I borrow many tears from these;
the underlying wash of sunken sailors
beneath the great lake's shining face,
the very breast-milk of rain,
the death breath of coal that flutters curtains
above the register under the window
we haunt for rumors of yellow

or

at least,

orange

but in gray, there is a

sinking

to —

Mustn't go there yet, not yet, too soon

We give lovers our roses, paint their lips,
valentine them with the passion of red,
but while we dance with life in bed,
in kitchens, in hidden blush of lust,
the kings menstruate on battlefields
and the sons of the poor paint the land
with the tyranny of crimson, and rivers of this
resist the eyes of sheep, who do not flee
from these mad jesters who so obscure
the stain they paint on man, the wasted eggs

and we

call

these

painters

god

Our minds must be blue; the hue we paint on sky,
on water, a color to clarify depth, the death of limits
We are all but scraps of stars, that unreachable yellow,
floating in the deepest blue we can look into
as if that coldest color holds all the secrets
We look for our fellows with blue eyes

and male painters

claim

blue

periods

Brown does not boast of thunderous umber
but raises the stalks of flower, sheaf of wheat,
hides the holy of germination, the birth of rivers,
hides, finally, our dead, beneath the skin
of a raped mother, a scorned home, a church,
buried beneath the concrete of crapping cretins

resolved

to

poison

grace

But, I, my eye, paint it all in black ink,
the nomenclature of a suicidal species
The poems will never be finished
until I finish the gray spiral into
that final color
and reams of dead children collect dust
in a multicolored room, beneath the detritus
of musician, artist, and the other miscreants

who

colored

my

world

looking for yellow

Impending

Oh, death, you great black bloom,
that writhes within my frame,
what name must I give you?

Are you the death of verse that looms
in remnant ears, the fear of silence?

Are you silence itself,
reverberating in the ear
of comrade left behind?
Oh, so drear, this impending quietude,
this large and final death.

We were birthed by stars,
and danced like holy dervishes
that feel the pull of sun,
and that grace of earth's own song
lightened the strides of decades
that brought the reaper near.

Will I gnash my worn teeth
and lash out at nonexistent gods
or think of daisies on fresh-turned earth,
rebirth to a form that needs not form?

But in some shining extacy,
in some Xanadu, populated by
peaceful wraith, there is no need of salve
for the victim of war, the bruised woman,
the serf of war-like king, no need
to apply the poultice of words
to herds of lemmings or sheep,
no need of poems,

no need of me.

Perhaps, the worms...

"To die, to sleep -
To sleep, perchance to dream - ay, there's the rub,
For in that sleep of death what dreams may come,
When we have shuffled off this mortal coil,
Must give us pause; " ... Hamlet: III i ll 63-7.

Oak

The man was only a man, and the oak, but a tree.
The morning blaze bid gray hair sing silver
and mouse-ear buds whisper green.

It was the river that looped a sacred mantra,
giggling its mysteries in the fine voice
of water over stone, murmurs of forever.

The old man, rooted to the Sioux by the soles
of his rubber river pants, plied the clear waters,
waving at the sky to send a gossamer thread -

in search of rising rainbows, bulging with eggs.
He looked at the ancient tree; feet, wet like his -
two broken branches, devoid of bud, home to many.

Oak had spent a lifetime, reaching from earth to sky,
knitting the elements with its hungry girth,
and he pondered his own withered limbs.

But oak was decomposing, grandchildren already
fed on his fine bones, morels, ferns, wild asparagus
gathered 'round his feet, greedy supplicants.

Seedlings gather to hear his stories, to thrive
as their grand spring echoes in the autumn
of an ageless tree, an aging fisherman.

The fisherman is a poet, reading his sprouts
stories about circles, about seasons and tides,
as he rides a rocking chair - crafted of oak.

Streets I walk with Marc

(for Marc Creamore)

Tiny urchins sell pussy on 42nd street
and the Dharma bums chant mantras from yellowed pages
between the nicotine fingers of the damned,
the ghosts that inhabit the echoes of collective consciousness,
denounced by the corporation behind the curtain.
I rail against the failed nomenclature of the merchant,
couched in the wry Dick and Janes who usurped
the bastion of of the beats with such thin stanzas,
indicative of a deeper sort of rot than dead soldiers describe.
What of Langston, of Jack and Jerry, of Allen and Robert Bly?
The sky is still the sky and we were all still crafted of stars.
Oh yes, and the scars,
the scars on the face of the red man's land; dead lakes
and oil wells, casinos, the modern smallpox blankets,
dotting the reservations like corporate scabs -
young black men, broken in battle to relieve brown men of oil -
'cause, if you can't play ball, it's either serve crack
at the corner or sign up at the mercenary's barracks
and get a gun to mow down Muslims, amen -
the old gods are dead, and the Stockholm Syndrome plays out
in churches in the South end of town, on the Rez,
and the rainbow marches off to war for Jesus -
Mississippi is still Mississippi, and the bruises still show,
Unkle Sam's a hungry motherfucker, and the poor gots to go!
The scars still show on the women, the very queens
who know that men should not kill men, and children
are not fodder for the war machines, but gracious gifts
of the moon, a playful nation of hope and glee.
The city sings of scars at midnight -
the urban blight that so inflames the predators, gleams
in the neon teeth that gnaw at the feral tribe of failures,
the broken soldiers, napalmed into refrigerator boxes
beneath the overpass, the flotsam and jetsam of capitalism
gone awry, the mother that cries for her broken girl,
wearing the pearl necklace of a twenty-dollar John,
two blocks south of the glittering palaces of the kings -
Oh, freedom, that used to ring so clear, shed light

in the alley, where the only common denominator is fear,
before the plight of the few is the cemetery of hope,
and we are all just rats on the treadmill of commerce.
Tom still sings, and Ani still insists, we must resist
the chains of such foolish masters, show our scars to the
tools of the fools in charge, the sheep that follow
charlatans beneath the wheels of war machines, and
profit machines, party monsters that crush the proletariat
beneath the wheels of injustice and greed.
Oh, scars, Oh bruised slave that yet stoops beneath the weight
of masters that will not share the American dream -
but every nightmare, every gun, every drug that keeps them quiet -
Oh woman, who blasphemes a mother's breast with
silicone and shame, powerless beneath the weight
of a sweating business man with all his blue pills and dollars -
Oh child, who must reap what we have sown, we fail you so.

Once, I walked streets full of mad jesters, flower wearing lovers
that knew the score in this game of life, pranksters that
practiced buffoonery in the face of war-mongers and thieves,
poets that poured truth over power to blunt the beast
to the jingle of finger-cymbals, the rhythm of flutes and drums,
the subliminal song of hope in a world gone mad.
I emptied my pockets to feed the poor, and knew what it felt
like to be rich, emptied my mind of dogma and shame
to enflame myself with the shared beat of one ginourmous tribe,
to chant in hopes of levitating the pentagon from mother's face,
and attaining a sort of grace devoid in stained glass mirrors.
Just yesterday, I heard a tired voice from the North, holding forth
on holy subjects, beyond the ken of gather-men and princes.

Marc sings like tarnished temple bells, pealing in the night,
in the autumn of a failed species, gasping like us, in the grip
of dollars and poems about nothing much, with small words,
from small minds that publish small verses in small journals
that avoid truth, adjectives, and bigger minds than Billy's.
He writes psalms for lovers that need no war or church,
no stack of currency to feel rich, but only love.
He writes books for the few who need him to renew our faith
in ourselves, for the few who would BE god, who know
that the flower is god, the butterfly is god, the river, the
Muslim, the black man, the queen in the gown and testicles,
the woman with the shopping cart full of cats,

the rats and other vermin, hell, even the Germans,
the bureaucrats, behind their desks,
and politicions, behind their masks, the soldier
who attacks for his nation's quest for more,
that little whore on 42nd street, shivering with need,
the farmers who feed the body electric,
the junky, stealing for a fix, the butcher, the baker,
the bread, the wheat, the soil, the oil that spills from
dinosaurs the sun forgot, the cloud that blots
the sun's face with rain, oh yeah, especially the rain,
the old oak tree that blocks the mansion's view, the maize,
the hippy from Nazareth, the fat man from the East,
every bird, every man and beast, the very land, ALL GOD.

Oh, Marc, with your voice of scars and hope,
with your stanzas burning so bright with sorrow and glee,
ask not for whom you write -
you write for me -

and if you bid us adieu before my days are through,
and my feeble pen yet sings,
then, brother, I'll write for you...

To Die Like a Baby

i want to die like a baby
secure in the wrong of ending
and the rising sun
of evermore

a beginning, a bright new
birth

Notes on morning's very song

The symphony begins with flutes
warbling the sun aloft
The blackbird, red-winged atop
a cattail throne -
the wee bumblebird
with flower-feet, pollen leggings
at the softest ballet -
droning in harmony with the button
on a string chorus of humming
birds, tiny tuning forks -
vibrating in teaspoon nests -
the alluring ardor
of bells and frogs -
the quickening of iris and thistle

The rustle of morels and wild
asparagus, waking beneath the
first green under mother's skirt
alerts the serenaders -
spring has unwound the thread
of winter's cloak

I fly through all on vulture's wings -
primaries whistling in the breath
of a god that needs no church
and the citizens of the sky
ply my eyes with color -
butterflies, waft like spring leaves
through the song of lark
and loon-flutes reverberate
over calm waters

In the old-man-tree
there are seventeen choirs
and baby bandits open their eyes
to a glittering world

I am born each morning
as my family sings
to fly on borrowed wings

Splattered Ink

 I heard my grace splatter
on the ties of the trestle.
It was a long way down
to this cube, this placenta.

I knew that god was but a dog
spelled backward by some
man in a placid pool.

I knew then - you are not real
and all my festivities
are only bad poems
that I wrote myself.

A Dog's Life

The stream appeared to drink the very sky
as if some vast dog spelled backward panted,
each face, each leaf, replete with moist supply
of silent psalms some spirit cloud granted.
Thank not for this, some distant mirror-god
with reverential flocks of beaming sheep,
or with a steepled, imposing facade
where black robed heroes and dank devils creep.
The sun and moon, the stars, are truly blessed,
and the bipedal saints we conjure, moot.
They set us to an impossible test,
passing a platter to collect their loot.

I think I'll make a god of my own dog,
or, perhaps, craft her of jubilant fog.

Ancient Springs

When springtime arrives
in the autumn
as a river seeks the sea
an old man ponders
trout, and the rust
on the earth's bones
Gravity will have its day
and glee, its repose
but for today,
he smiles

After the fire, after
the ice, comes calving
time, the thaw, and the
very earth softens
to accept a poet

He wrote a poem for
an origami boat,
floated it away
in the arms of the Sioux,
and titled it
"Notes for Mississippi"
as the spring flood
carried him
to the sea -

to the albatross

Autumn Love

To love a girl is most sublime,
to see your future in her eyes
as bodies writhe in perfect rhyme
with song of moon, with her sighs.

To love a woman is holy,
to plant a garden with your love
and trust the fruit of a lowly
man to the womb of such a dove.

To love a lovely crone transcends
the momentary glee of man
as autumn's warm colors descend
in an hourglass, short of sand.

To love a crone is bliss indeed
as the grave waits to intercede.

Soiled Angels with Poet

He dined in the shelter of doom,
with Baudelaire and Poe,
such dark company
where whiter angels
fear to feed.

His ink, replete with phantoms
spilled in ochre smears
like mascara from
some deity's
tears -

sings dirges of diseased damsels,
and the great black heart
pumps such verses
that sooty angels
swoon.

The Absence of Furies

(for Anne Sexton)

Someone trembles in the dark
remembering her breath
on his neck, whispering
"Always, baby, always..."
in a holy spasm
They sent a monkey into space
but they amputated his hands
so he wouldn't push
her buttons, and yet, he itched
I'm sure of that
He fumbled for her button
in the dark, flicked it off
when she made him
what she thought she
wanted
and an untamed monkey pirate
moistened her resolve
perhaps Sylvia, in monkey skins
or a psychiatrist, laying on hands
in the absence of god's caress

It is all about the zoo, you see
the pacing, the masturbating monkey
the tigress on her throne of straw
the faces and faces
streaming by in a rictus of grins
and jeers, the fear, the feces
But she closed the zoo
when god ate her cub
with desperate teeth and songs
The organ grinder
of cities and cities amputated her heart
and the transplant didn't love him,
didn't nurse remaining cub
and always whispered
from the tail pipe

Someone trembles in the dark
remembering Anne

Notes from a Hermit

Sometimes, I feel like the punch-line of some vast cosmic joke, a reminiscence from
some mad jester, some paisleyed prankster. The prairie, the forest beyond my window,
seem, but constructs of a ravenous mind. The dogs at play, the garden, the children,
grandchildren, the penis I follow in its quest for some warm, moist, holy test; the very
she of moon, of stars, of womb; this very skeleton, seem but infatuations of a loving
mind. But, why do I make them hurt me so?
I wonder if I invented centuries of poets to measure myself by. I wonder why Sam
invented a better Xanadu than I. I wonder why Allen didn't make me gay, despite the
craving for Liz, for Sylvia and Anne, for that ultimate three-way. I wonder why Jack
doesn't come back to hang out. I wonder why, given the verbose company I keep, I'm
such a hack. I wonder why I left the freeway of the rails to settle into this mask of
conformity and commerce, why I crafted this texture of wars and homeless heroes, this
fabric of an Amerika, bereft of Walt's dungareed farmers, his strong women; this
bastion of corporation and shame.
I sit by the Sioux, my church, and wonder if this song of water over stone is only a
manifestation of my need for gravity, if that chrome and crimson trout that climbs the
falls is me, missing tie-dyes. I pout, I ponder on such meaningless nouns, that clowns
in my id dance 'round a maypole with flapping feet. I greet the very sunrise with
skepticism, retreat from that vast splendor to the future funeral for the light. I writhe
in daymares of my own design. I should have made myself happy.

Never Mind Actual Poetry

Mind the boxes of flags and religious paraphernalia.
Mind the slobbering fervor of Texas republicans
    or the Dick and Jane march of diligent academics.
Mind the tedious flood of engorged sweatpants
    populating tea-bag parties and the aisles
    of the collective Wal Mart.
Mind the Billy Collins clones, holding court in every
    MFA program in every corporate educational bastion
    of uni-syllabic prose poetry in Amerika!
Mind the pursed and wrinkled lips that whisper
    "Show, don't tell!" "Don't use adjectives or rhyme!"
    or "Shut the fuck up about politics and war!"
REMEMBER, use wee words; poets are not to grow language,
    but shrink it to fit the small minds of the merchant-class.
Mind the pablum of dancing stars, of repugnant
    and dim foxes and American idols of plastic
    shrink wrap, saline breasts that do not suckle tomorrow,
    but only sell insurance, large automobiles, and Viagra.

Never mind the albatross, the road not taken, dreams
    of Xanadu, the body electric, the music of ardent word,
    follow the herd to rivers never fished, to thin lines
    that smell like catfish bait, the schemes of millionaires
    that read on public radio for pseudo intellectuals
    that vote for pseudo liberals in pseudo elections.
    As long as wealthy white men can get erections, life
    will be groovy in this vast geography of lemmings.
Never mind the whales or women in the Congo, ya know,
    they ain't got no oil anyway: they don't vote in Ohio.
Never mind that the US poet-laureate is Eastern European,
    as long as he toes the conservative line like Billy.
Never mind the corporation behind the curtain, sending
    the young of the poor to troll for oil with blood-bait,
    or the war-criminal on the news, redefining patriotism
    to fit between the gears of his own war machine,
    or his puppet in the big white mansion, selling
    the lemmings to the doctors that bleed them for every
    cent before they give them a permit to die, amen.

Never mind the men who sell their votes, the pre-determined
    elections, the erection of monuments to criminals.
Never mind the slam poets that remember Sam, that howl
    like Allen or Larry, the very voices of revolution;
    submit to the evolution of poets to the kingdom of the bland,
    the land of prose poetry with a little wry humor.

Mind the academics; write small box-shaped poems about
    nothing much, about apple-pie and ice-cream, about
    the Amerikan dream for the "right" children of the "right"
    fathers, of the proud democracy, by the wealthy, for the wealthy,
    and don't ever forget that professors and editors are wealthy.
    As long as we keep THEM healthy, everything will be fine.

Never mind rumors and signs of apocalypse, dead kids
    on desert sands, mercenaries in lock step, marching us all
    to oblivion; we are lemmings after-all, and it is the job,
    the duty of poets, to paint a yellow brick road to the
    very edge of the cliff,
    and to make them like it.

Never mind - Jack Kerouac

Screaming With Baudelaire

Oh, you wurst of poet-meat and gut,
lost love,
desist in painting shame so clear
that blame is worn like
paisley in a crowd
in dowdy canvas -

release my pen from the dinge
of Baudelaire, the rictus-faced screams
you bring to the fevered dreams of poets -

release me from ghost-breasts
and thorn of rosy lip,
to write my way
to morning

Nightmares

There are soldiers in my head,
hiding behind orders and Humpty Dumpty.
They put down Mc spatulas
to burn brighter than napalm
and decorate themselves
with merit badges for carnage
and a mercenary's purse.

Allen is dead, and Billy flings feces
into the collective of puerile saints
that read white noise
but all I see is the skeletal man
who really did fish the Susquehanna.

Baudelaire knew, as did Sam and Edgar
that nightmares are the grist of
larger wheels than Dick, Jane,
or Billy will ever spin, but the son
has set on Patterson, and the steed
that took us further rots
in a California pasture.

In my dreams, my poems,
a fetus climbs out of a dumpster
to end all the wars and clean tainted rivers,
while the homeless are moved in
to the mansions of bloated leeches,
vampires at the diner of labor's vein.

Flowers die at midnight
like vinyl daisies the chimp's apprentice
trickled down on, and does yet.
I see ranks of marching eights,
battalions of them keeping pace
with a closeted body-builder
in California with earthquakes.

I see Dubya in blackface,
giving Johnny another gun,
with six million excuses
to fatten a calf for Johnny's corpse.

In my nightmares, I see America burning.

Did you ever awaken from a nightmare
to see the same dank visions awake,
to see poverty poets and wealthy soldiers
with necklaces of ears, to see the sun
blotted out by mother's tears, and a holy fetus
climbing back into a dumpster?

I did.

The end...

The Chair

An empty chair rides a weathered porch
on a night dark as Baudelaire's flowers.
Another poet has passed the verbose torch.

He rocked out there for countless hours,
nursing nouns and verbs to dance like lovers,
to salve society; to throw the truth at power.

While children slept beneath their covers,
he fought monsters with verses of words,
and around that old chair, a poet still hovers.

From milk of human kindness, he made curds
as if the gist of wholesome thought grew cheese.
He made the simplest phrases fly like birds.

He wrote of love and gentle folk of the land,
of miracle of rising sun, of generosity, and bliss,
but society showed him the back of its bloody hand

and his last verse floated away on pink mist.

Death in Chicago

Hellbound, broken-hearted beneath the wheels of love
he dredged the depths of mean streets for an out
Imbued with hues of bluest tinge and straight-razor
streets, big windy was happy to oblige
He traded the south-side shotgun shack for the ooze
of festering hearts in the neon battlefield
where battalions of wolves prowled the urban wilderness

The eyes of Chicago would see him die
the feral children, selling bodies at the crack of midnight
the hip-shot whore under mercury's merciless glare
the pimp, hungry for the fruit of diseased vine
the old woman in nine sweaters, her cat from his throne
in the shopping cart, full of the merchant's guilt
the suicidal white boy, buying a death rock
from a black boy that serves it, devoid of options
the peroxide blond, with two o'clock mascara
running like a watercolor of grease on canvas of shame
to reach herpes lips that yawn wide like the
desperate grin of a corpse that got the joke she didn't
the hero that peeks from the mouth of a Maytag cave
the closing-time secretary, in the long-sleeved dress
that hid the scars that made her real when she was alone
the black-jacketed pirate that would keep her from cutting
tonight, for a taste of her darkest fears, the very heart
of night, the big blue moon that would witness all
the man with a peroxide blond girlfriend and a 9mm
the rats

Like many an inner storm
this one ended with the sound of thunder
and the voice of a blue guitar

Estuary, a Love Story

I came to the North on the verge of many things. It seemed, as I trod
my new geography, fitting that the lake rode the red shoulders of the
land like a mysterious blanket, leading to unseen places called
"Thunder Bay", and "Silver Bay", sights like twenty-one Apostles,
emerald mountains rising from clear depths to claim a taste of sky.
Everywhere, the sound of drumbeat, from the dancing circles,
connecting a people to a place by way of eager feet and open hearts,
atop red cliffs, to the grouse, sounding so like a distant two-cylinder
Deere, pounding the very air to seek a mate, to, finally, my first
experience of the slow beat of tide, the heartbeat of moon. I followed
these to the Sioux.

They say it takes a steelhead to catch one, and the first time I broke
through the snow to stand in the rush of winter's death, to hear the
finger-cymbals of this singing stream, I swung wide those creaking
hinges of closed mind to drink it, to soften my hard mind.
The first roll of trout, exposing chrome and lipstick flank, introduced
me to a new sort of neon, the bright light of sun on a standing wave, the
very determination of a circle of water reaching from sky to earth, to
river, to inland sea, the determination of trout to climb any waterfall to
answer life's call. I climbed the clear river down, down to the estuary,
the fecund mergence of forest, stream, and the great mystery of
Superior.

Others call this waypoint of a river's journey swamp, and with the
effort of this bottomland to suck the waders from me, I must agree. But
more, this verge, this undecided marriage of stream, to forest and
endless lake, is a wildlife singles-bar, a moist dance-floor, and finally,
the richest nursery on mother-nature's smiling face. The drone of a
million-million insects, living tiny lives at the speed of sound, the
minnows, the tiny ducks, the red-winged black-bird on a cattail throne,
the turtles, painted on stones to plop
into the world beneath my gaze as I splash by, the pine-filtered light
that fastens itself
to a thousand micro-worlds at once, the countless voices that sing a
symphony of a place where everything joins everything.

I climbed countless granite Rushmores from stream to sky, to spy faces of other dreamers in the clouds, sank into clear waters to cleanse myself of the long day's commerce and struggle, dunked myself in deeper waters in a church with steeples of pine.
I dined on the citizens of the land, given to my arrows like meals from that ruthless and wonderful supermarket of earth, the closing of circles, cured myself at the apothecary
of fern and wintergreen, ginseng and rain, grew my garden at the headwaters of the Sioux.

I would marry a girl raised by the Namekagon, a green-eyed child of the boreal forest.
North, we would flee, to the great divide to join the joining of elements, that the circle remain unbroken, and our cycles know the gentle reminder of tide. Laughter would be our song, and our children would grow at the headwaters of my favorite stream, the stream of my own consciousness. They would be the children of the Sioux.

Writing with Rimbaud's Ghost

The night writes with black ink
Rimbaud's wolves run through
my pen in search of the sound
of carrion

Harnessed to a ghost, I write
on the unraveling velvet
of night

Trio

Wolf

My hackles rise when wolf-song rings,
when grizzled hunters split the night,
as if my very spirit sings
to spur the deer to frightened flight.

My eye-teeth even seem to grow
in response to jubilant howl,
feet curl, in sleep, to grip the snow,
and, dreaming, my muse starts to prowl.

Midnight

I so adore the wolf, in fur and song,
as scores of voices split the night
to sing the plight of stag.

As winter's dark paints snow so blue
and deer are put to flight by wraiths
that paint the land in crimson -

a raven croons his sing-song call
in the light of a perfect circle.

Run

Run, you king of midnight sun,
that so ignites this poet's pen:
I hear you sing the moon aloft again,
and delight in the hunter's voice.

As if the very night is yours alone,
you rejoice in your meat-song,
and the flight of the deer
is imagined - as the poet runs along.

The edge

"There is no honest way to explain it
because the only people who really know
where it is are the ones who have gone over"

Dr. Gonzo - Hunter S. Thompson

What is a Poet?

We're just folks, you see.
Oh, yeah, we shit, we fuck, we watch TV
and pluck our eyebrows, we brow-beat sullen
artichokes with sonnets and balsamic acid,
greet our spouses with ceremony kisses and lies,
as if daffodils were real: we really hate said
daffodil for its insect life, its surge of impermanence,
its short-term bliss.

We're the ones that fell off the edge of the world
and came back with stories, verses of Albatross
and rose, of a kiss, an illegal, immoral, enlightened kiss
with metaphor twining with rapturous tongue
in pursuit of such naked song that angels rasp it
like that broken bird from Texas.

Sheep will not grasp the fleetest of us, will bleat
at descriptive phrasing of genitalia and kings,
but wolves and open minds will sing along.

We will not fear those kings or armies of their
over-compensating concubines in their matching outfits,
prancing with guns and necklaces of ears,
but shine our verbose light on each monster
that seeks to eat the meat of other-colored man,
that reeks of shame of arming the meek
to fill the treasure troves of the damned.

We, the proud patriots of poetry
carry the flag of love
into the battle for the human spirit,
and understand that guns are for shooting
stubborn typewriters.

Tainted Cinderellas

You see them everywhere:
   the Barbie that siliconed her fortune
   to claw her way from the trailer
   to the Hollywood hills,
   but her mascara runs like
   the greyhound that brung her.
You see the ghetto boy with pigskin,
   movin' on up to mentor
   young men on fighting pits
   behind golden gates, the
rags to riches to ditches story, the
   tainted Cinderellas in castles
   of cocaine and excess, the
   broke-ass lottery winner
   with gun-oil breath.

You see them in court: in one or two gloves,
   devoid of shame or recompense,
   dancing in the flames of wealth
   that lick their feet like dire
   concubines in Dante's visions.

You see them in a duct-taped kitchen,
   in a closed garage, whispering last poems
   with the gaseous voice
   of Poe's raven,

   as you bask in the riches of the poor.

Notes on a Broken Mirror

I looked into the mirror to see who I am,
to look myself right in the eye.
My third eye opened with a resounding SLAM
to a man bereft of alibi.

In gloom of night, awash in thin silver sheen,
a wicked grimace faced the world,
as if Poe's raven sallied forth to preen
while a dire flag unfurled.

That mirror, that door, had painted me black,
as if every dark prophesy bloomed.
My rictus teeth, my bones, began to CLACK
as Dante's deepest darkness loomed.

My comrades, my fellows, had darkened my view:
they'd painted many sins on me.
Those hypocrites, those judges in the wooden pews
painted it black before I could flee.

They painted us into firefights for glory,
painted us into tiny boxes,
painted us wounds, most heinous and gory,
fed us to Australian foxes.

My third eye opened the mirror deeper,
to seek out a way to be free,
to be my own judge, to face that reaper,
to pick up a rock and FLEE!

When that false mirror shattered, I finally knew
that goodness comes in many hues.
So, I bought a new mirror
and painted it blue.

With an Angel on my Shoulder

i write winter's wondrous frost
i sing soft stanzas for tomorrow's ears
as if to string them brightly into sun

With a swan in mind
i surrender words to the vagaries of
gentle ears, lest i fail that test of time
and fade into dusty shelf of obscurity

With a brother in flutesong

to hold her dear, sing her free
she oversees my poetic destiny
with the glee of proud librarian
that keeper of most precious rhyme
that stands the test of time to sing
in the rarefied air of future

With softest touch of discipline
she calms my tones of ice and steel
with proper breadcrumbs on that
twisting trail to books and ears
that so befuddles my crude pen -

again, and yet again
she cleans my verbose children
for presentation to the eyes
of a larger world

if ever i weave a pattern of words
a bandage of earnest verse
to heal the future of war

Wanda will be the seamstress
to make them fit

To Howl in Harmony with Ghosts

Into the pages of sages
that ruffled in the fire-breath of wars
Into elevated nomenclature of minstrels
that sing the universe of men, the cancers
of flag and cannon that obscure light

Load the ammunition of ancient scribes
Load the diatribes of word's dead hero
Load the circles of moon and dancing tribes
to the pen of today's wordslinger, and breach
the stone-faced libraries with bravest truth

FOR OUR COMRADES
that haunt the open mind from repository
of dust and silence, from forgotten shelves
where the voices of ghost-poets yet resound
we raise today's sharp sword, eager quill
to still the sound of battle, to write
in harmony with poets that knew
that we must write a path to peace
to belie the battle cry of greedy kings

and thus renew our pact
with eons of poets
that inseminated us
with the language
of heroes

Tigress

You stalk my years with feline grace
burning in my eyes like morning
We have danced like leaves
in many winds, bloomed like lotus

We germinated in flowered fields
to strains of northwind and loon

You opened for me like river for stream
I drank of you, and you of me
as we flowed through our forest of years
laughing like water over stones

November Rain

Whether we wither like
leaves that have fled to
skies of lead and thunder
or orange ourselves with song,
when the third breath of autumn sings
we cringe.

IMPINGE! IMPINGE! O North
that sings of naked bone,
it's much too early
to call me home -

and such warm colors jubilate
that aging suitors court the moon
with cedar voice of loon
and silver whiskers croon to
anoint the eyes of young
with vistas of story.

It's true; winter will have its due,
but poets and dancers are hewn of fire
and warmer hues cut the murk
where blank-faced granite lurks
to paint November orange.

On Broken Eggs

He would have seen the flowers
with first-open-eyes -
would have played like a dervish
until loving time and tasks.

He may have written immortal verse -
devoid of pragmatic curse and deed.
But for the flensing knives of greed,
I name him poet, lover, father.

Should his womb have cherished
him in rapture and magic,
had readied him for breath,
he would have sung.

My son, my god, my innocence,
were murdered in August.

Funeral Suit

When I've worn out
my suit of words
and I've breathed my last poem
into ear of finest crone...

sprinkle me on the garden
till me deep
and clothe me in robust
vegetables

Bloodstains on the Yellow-Brick-Road

As if there had been no war
   I imagine Johnny in Canada
   in one piece and dancing
   away from the reality
   of his gun, his nightmares
   the orange fetus that put
   his mind on the north wall
As if there had been no war
   we wipe our minds clean
   with bloody flags and hero songs
   while butterflies migrate
   thousands of miles to paint
   the sky with animate leaves
   and we leave teeth beneath pillows
As if there were no broken folks
   that invoke midnight screams
   we plant into the small moon
   and spill seeds on Betty-Lou's
   alabaster to raise the son
   of Jesus that demands blood
   in the name of his distant geography
   that speaks through the forked
   tongues of ravens that eschew grace
As if pigs could fly, we wage war for peace
As if a breast had a trigger, we kill
   to get into Sally's bloomers
   with uniforms and shrieking anthems
   but you can't nurse a child with an M-16
As if peace were not repugnant to kings
   we lower our eyes from moon
   to a black liar with red hands
   and call ourselves patriot for
   ignoring the color of things
As if the wealthy can't bleed, we nominate
   the poor to kill and die so the sons
   of kings may recreate in Betty-Lou
   while the burger-flippers fry Muslims
   for Zionists beneath a hotter sun
As if there were enough flowers for all the
graves we grace our eyes with purple
mountain'smajesty, lower taxes on leeches

so generals can all
  have 38DDD wives to suck the sin from them
  so they can ride blue pills to oblivion
  over the bodies of serfs that get
  higher taxes and decorated corpses
As if we are not at war, I paint my eyes
  with the shades of peace, with flutesong
  to drown out the din of anthems and bass
As if our mother had not intended for murderers
  to claim the evolutionary prize, I try to pry
  my brother's eyes from mayhem and gore
  from prophets and profits, from hero to poet
  from Iraq, Pakistan, Afghanistan, from Iran
  to the tan-line that frames a human breast
  to the daily miracle of son, the dreams of moon
  to the very land that feeds us from beneath
  the skin of this glorious blue ball
As if we learned the first lesson from the first mother
  of the first man, I pretend that I am not
  a disease, but a lover, and I will count no coup
  for an evil clown in a red-white-and blue
  top hat and his fucktard minions

  forever

The YEEEHAAW! People

are snapping synapse, sparkling
like stars on a black-velvet
Elvis painting
are dynamos of surveillance
observers of imaginary gods
the clitoris and everything
with songs for spoiled meat
and daffodils
with Georgia's flower bone sex
and a sunburst of glees -
savage in their needs

are trickster, like Ojibway fox
are lightning at sunset, are fire
that burns for each new morning

and breaks like crystal at love
are broken sparrows
and that jubilant scream of birth
are dead junkies with callused
guitar fingers, bleeding
the blues into new decades
for lovers that burn to cinder
and hobos on a boxcar
that flies into thirty shades of gray
are midnight whistles
lubricated by mourning dew
are glue of orgasm and pain
at the center of everything
are motion in a static nation
are the geographers of the mind
are laughing too hard
loving too loud
crying like wet cats
and telling demon truth
with the voices of clouds
are the thin screech of fingernails
on blackboards in Tangiers
and Colorado, in Patterson
on the soft folds of frontal lobe
and the very abode of gods
are the stanzas of poets
with testicles, breasts, and excess
are oiling the next albatross
with a big YEEEHAAW!

am such
am maladroit juggler of words
and colors, with ten-thousand
rhymes, ten-thousand tears
ten thousand *hallelujahs*
am dew and hail, sunshine and grace
am doom like every war
and thunder before storm
am flower and bone
am god and monster
am poet
am burning
burning

Universal Soldier

(For Buffy St. Marie)

I'm just a man in the throes of decay
in the land of decaying airwaves
I dug my grave with things
that plug me in to empty eye-sockets
of war's automatons, reeking soldiers

I'm the proud rapist of my mother
that tries to wipe off the blood
with flags

I dissect families from afar, name
myself hero to pin medals
on midnight screams, because I
scored a touchdown on the field
of battle, painted my nights
with dreams of patriotic gore
for a greatful nation

I take off my infected uniform
to poke a saber into Betty-Lou
to the beat of anthems, the march
to impregnate the spoils of war

Betty-Lou weeps at the blood
on the evening news
and names herself
blameless

I Am America

In my jack-boots and blood salute,
in my churches, in my burning churches
and diamond synagogues heated by missiles.

I am the quarterback that stains white cotton
with blood for Mary Jane and flags.
I am dirty munitions, the pride of spinning bullet,
the cries of first nation children, the fox
fleecing the sheep for monstrous appetites.

I am burning coal and wheezing poets,
proms and prams with shining twins,
apple-pie, cartoons, cartons of mother's milk
with victim faces, cars, millions of cars
and carrion.

I'm the farmer though, the carpenter,
the baker of pies, the lover, the saint
in the soup kitchen, serving up hope,
the eloping angels, awash in love,
the red mother, dancing to skin drums
in circles that valiantly dispute cubes,
the working mother in the wake
of the dashing penis in the red convertible
that flew off to dissect Muslims
for the ol' red, white, and blue.

I'm Monsanto, with troves of cash and
deformed fetuses, wrapped in our flag.
I'm that hippy that reminds the soldier
that he can't hide dead children under levels
of orders, orders from filthy old men that
order bodies like those young fools
order burgers from Mickey-fucking D.

I am the field artillery, singing anthems
of pride, to a back-beat of bombs

shredding rice and families in Viet-Nam,
shredding innocents so oil-rich kings
won't shred innocents and one guy won't
call Dubya's daddy names in Halliburton's
Iraq; I'm a bullet buried at Wounded - Knee,
a musket-ball in an Iroquois burial mound,
exposed to the eyes of round tourists,
that stalk the aisles of Wal Mart in
over-burdened sweatpants at noon on Monday.

But I'm still in tie-dyes, playing a cedar flute
to win love in a time of carnage, to fill the air
with human birdsong to drown out the screams.

I'm the broken young man that awoke from
dreams of glory to see he has shed a limb
to feed a beast that lied to him.

I am, at heart, a mother, who only wants
to live a dream usurped by most unwholesome king,
usurped by men who covet power and geography,
by men who eat their young like jackals
because the sheep they marry succumb to wolf.

It is time, IT IS TIME! IT IS TIME!
for the sheep to bleat, for the meek
to claim the prize of America,
to wrench the seat of power from greedy men
in the final hour of a gasping nation,
to fling the loudest truth on the steps
of every library, every courthouse,
every electronic glimmer of airwaves,
that we are a nation of mothers,
that we CAN make America America again.

We stopped the war in 73
We did it once, we can do it again.
Compliancy is no longer an option
when the wolf gnaws at the door.

I am America, and I'm finally waking up.

PEEKABOO!

*"I'm just a human being with a lot of
shit on my heart"*

(Jack Kerouac, from "The Goofball Blues")

I first became aware of the great mystery playing peekaboo
    in a pissant shotgun shack in a pissant
    farm town with a wheel-dingered Texaco, a church,
    a drug store with penny candy, and two bars
    in the endless corn of Illinois
I wore my Vitalis-varnished hair and my little suit to Sunday school
    where god lived with rules and damnation
    as if a child could carry the weight of hell
    to school come Monday - in a little tin
    Batman lunchbox with baloney and bovine milk
Others of my ilk sang hymns, "YES, JESUS LOOOVES ME"
    but I shivered beneath my covers lest I be judged
    as fuel for an inferno of my own device
    as I played like a jubilant little pagan
    that understood that the man who planted
    that burlap bag of puppies in the stream
    that carried my innocence down to the Mississippi,
    down to the fecund delta, and to the sea
    would be forgiven - with the right name
    on his dying lips - - - but not me
I was, you see, too young to be bereft of blinders, too young
    to cheat so at this game of peekaboo.
I was, you see, the child that WANTED to be the Indian,
    as the other boys rode brooms, "YEEHAWED"
    as they blasted rolls of snap to blood me,
    the child that poked a bag with a stick
    and spelled god backward at the tumble
    of grace into that muddy stream of conscience
You see, the only man in town with beagles was the pastor

I heard ghostly voices from Patterson, in gray New Jersey,
    from Tangiers, heard the Mexico City Blues in discordant

polkas and electric anthems from a black man with
a white strat, wailing voices from bruised Mississippi,
and chants from mountains that lived where
my sun was born of infinite sky,
I heard Little Bobby Zimmerman whine nasal
brilliance after he left iron Minnesota
for the truth, whispered in the raspy voice of New York
I heard Martin show the way to the mountain's majesty
and the righteous screams of panthers in the night,
fighting with all their might to be seen as men

I heard the song of the moon sing from white cotton wrappers
that I would for decades try to ply with a Cheshire Cat grin

"PEEKABOO!"

Every girl, each woman, has her own secret rhythm, her own
harmony with moontide, with sunrise, with aboriginal drums
that beat in circles wherever that East wind blows,
her own secret dance, and Mars fell under the spell of Venus
to the throb of menses and the swell of mother's protruberance
I germinated at the first sight of breast-bud, bloomed, at the
first faint touch of mystery-fur, swooned when I first
provoked the holy circling of a girl's soft hips,
and I knew what "YEEHAWS" were for, and
I decided that my church lived in a woman's arms
that held me tight to simpler sorts of truth

"PEEKABOO!"

While I was busy growing hair and hair-brained ideas of love
the king was sending serfs to war for French dollars
on the other side of the circle, Monsanto was
oranging fetuses, deforesting strings of genes
for the almighty green, and the napalm barbeque
smelled funky all the way to Illinois
I put down Lao Tzu, Nixon, and other proponents of military to pursue
hippy chicks with ideals and breasts, with full knowledge
that if I but follow the downy grail of woman,
that yellow brick road, that mushroom-scented target
would lead me to the right sort of dog
I wore the road-dust and tie-dyes of a non-conformist, the uniform

of the patriot that would not bleed for angry flags,
The insane dynamo of cities ate farms like popcorn, waters
    grew mud, suds, and poison at the filthy hands of commerce
The wheels of progress were always lubed by
    the blood of first nations, nations that knew
    we must dance, must circle our tribes
    to defend the very sky from dragon-breath,
    who knew that gods anoint not the fountain with death
    or stain the spirit with the glint of gold
    where the light of night's diamonds should shine,
    who knew that sun and rain were holy

The sun rose over the Atlantic, cut through the pall of smoke
    on the Eastern seaboard to catch it's breath
    before it lit the oily gears of Chicago,
    before it witnessed the vast flat of corn and beans,
    the scream of pole-axed steers that was punctuated
    by the rockies, and, finally, set on the hope of Frisco
While my heart sought Ferlinghetti, my head read
    the Desiderata, but my ass belonged to Uncle Sam,
    just another chunk of Spam to be roasted in Viet Nam,
    but I fought my war with placards, cos my mamma
    taught me that my brother was not for killing
    and war was not holy,
    currency was not holy,
    and Buffy taught me that soldiers were no more
    holy than the kings that sent them to kill
The priests had their boys and vaults of gold, the preachers
    sent our boys to war from bloody pulpits
    while the nuns beat the language from red children,
    from brown children, from black and yellow children,
    as if this mission be ordained by the voice of gentle Jesus
My dog wore a bandana, played Frisbee, and humped with glee
    as god became irrelevant in drum circles,
    irrelevant on organic farms, at poetry readings,
    on the road that led irrevocably to nowhere
    because I was everyone's neighbor,
    everyone's field hand, lover, playmate, friend,
    and there were women in the ghetto,
    women on the farm, women in and behind bars,
    women who knew the secret names for stars,
    and god seemed a dim name for the womb of everything
    when nothing revealed itself as endless room

for enlightenment, devoid of doom or shame

"PEEKABOO!"

I found clearer waters on the North Coast of my America,
    found a woman that WAS holy, that flowed to me
    from the clean passage of the Namekagon
    that carved my way to bliss through boreal forest
I found the one true secret light enough for me to carry,
    that despite the thrust and parry of Venus and Mars
    it is the mothers who know the way to light
I tried to light the way for other men, to sing the song of peace,
    to thrust my spear of words into the black heart
    of war, to even the score for the meek,
    but the king sent his minions with guns,
    with charges of open eyes in the land of the blind,
    with charges of trying to usurp the throne
    of poisons and blood with a flood of ideas,
    and my liberty bell fell silent for twenty years
My garden, my good wife's arms, my children's laughter,
    were such a fine prison, such refuge as America died,
    that I was not wounded by the cancer at large,
    but meek, sharing my wooden voice with the loon,
    in hiding from the pincers and crusades
    of old men with angry gods leering from mirrors

"PEEKABOO"

Their wars leered at me from the entrancer screen, with
    holocaust breeding holocaust, breeding holocaust,
    in the name of the dogs that chased me through the decades
    of complacency and fear until I strapped on the pen
    of a wordslinger to try and clean up the Dodge City
    of a sick America, to Howl like Allen at the mainlining
    of violence by old white men who fill pockets with
    distant death, addicted to the rush of power over their betters
As my girl grew from sylph, to mother, to glow of crone,
    I honed my sword of words, as I must to earn the trust
    of such a wise daughter of the moon,
    because trust, you see, lubricates the gates of Venus,
    trust is not fostered by force of arms, by green scraps
    of monopoly money, by bloody flags or larger maps,
    and I quit the game of peekaboo as I must

in the garb of a grandfather, to tell the boys,
to pry their eyes away from the blinders of kings
and the false security of things, to the most simple truth
that heroes do not kill their fellows
and closed eyes cannot find the light

PEEKABOO!

The Rainy Day Polka

I fell too far

as if you are moon, I tide
and so drawn into your womb
that little self abides

Shorn of this, bereft of kiss
from the only lips that draw
me so like moth to flame
am I remiss in saving some self
for such a rainy day

Perhaps that bliss was nightshade
for such a lover as I, poison
that slid down smooth
like the face of broken glass

Now, the abyss stares into me
with your eyes

and all I really wanted
was a piece of ass

Hangin' with Freak

We were wild as a Nor-Easter
in the days of placards for peace,
when the breasts swung free,
and we laughed like madmen
at the sight of these.

*

I was his one phone call, and he, mine
when our dervishes ran amok.

*

We read the finest literature
of tracks, written across the forest,
the swamps and prairies,
beneath the tide-moon and stars,
and we made our meat.

*

When one of us was broken,
we had three legs to run with,
three arms to build.

*

He had a truck, and I, a chain,
he, a backbone, and I a brain.
We reverse this order on a regular basis
as a friendship is no place for stasis.

*

HE has no progeny, but WE have three.

*

Together, we make strong enemies,
beautiful friends, a landscape
of guffaws to light dark nights.

*

A friend is a brother whose mother
is not required to love you.

*

When I rain, he is the thunder to announce it.

*

When I have written my last love poem
he will care for her...

Soft Like This

It is soft like this
when something dies, when some
snow-laden bough snaps
no drama, no latent movie-of-the week or
angst-ridden screech
just a muted throb as the present is buried in
frigid limbo, in ponderous stasis
as the pines divest themselves
of a mother's frozen tears

Burial is softest clothed in such mantle
Flutes go silent, crushed, one, by one
between the blue gears of winter
and the poet, recumbent beneath his broken truck,
beneath the vast and silent weight of sky,
beneath the snow, beneath the notice of
gods or other vultures
welcomes the softest hush
of nevermore

When

my last poem rolls across the eye
   like water over stone
   and the last germ, last seed
   of word is nurtured by your mind
love them well, my jubilant children
   and press their flowers into books

When

the lines have all become too long for
   my meager breath to bestow
   sing them to the sprouts
   of other men, that I sing yet
after the last rain drinks my thunder
   and my final leaves have fallen

When

my compost is ripe, and heroes
   are made of the kind and meek
   I will quicken daisies, as once
   I quickened a golden girl, beneath
   the sun that pulls them so
beneath the moon
   that pulled me into you
beneath the stars
   your eyes hung high for me

When

You give me up to fire, as surely was
   my voice borne by this, and must I be
divide me thus - half for the garden
   that whispered so many secrets
   to my simple pen
   and half for the winds
   that howl and whisper like me

   (you know I always wanted to fly)

When

you miss me, as surely you attached
   too much of self to such a selfish bloom
listen, and you will hear me in the breeze

When I freeze you from the north
   remember that war was not real
   that the heart of man is not in this
   aberration of crooked growth
but it is merely a fungus, born of greed
   and the fits of diseased kings

When I caress you from the east, with
   peaceful breezes and bamboo flutes
   remember me with hibiscus
   and laughter at irony

When I ruffle your silken tresses from the west
   plant maize; plant beans and greens
   to rise like obscene laughter, dance
   in my growing arms once more
   like the fecund lovers we were
Listen for the sound of a courting flute
   and don't forget the flowers

When I shout from the south with lightning
   remember when I speared warriors
   with the gentle weapons of language
and teach them that placards are more holy
   than guns

ABOVE ALL

   don't forget to dance

Drops of Poisoned Rain

While he watched his top-soil
blow away with his seed
the farmer heard the bitch caterwaul
"DRILL BABY, DRILL"
and his tears dried too

  ***

Three white dots swim to nowhere
beyond the reach of ice
The smaller two remind me of my children
drowning beneath the waves
of corporate greed

  ***

Coastal cities beneath sea-level drown
and god shrugs

  ***

Bono flies on mega jets enough
to smother a small planet
with all his empty words
Ms Crow needs four eighteen wheelers
to sing, but she demands that I
give up toilet-paper

  ***

The "environmental president"
wants to sell the right to pollute

  ***

A poet makes a special trip to town
to infect the grid with poems
of an agrarian nature

  ***

The right-to-lifers support the wars

  ***

Nebraska

My Broken Hallelujah

(For Leonard)

I haven't found a name for god
so all the children of spirits bound
to dreaded acts of men in names of them
name me heretic, and name me odd.

I used to think his son was tossed
with nails, atop a wooden cross
so all my greatest sins could be forgiven
but his spokesmen are driven to war.

I think, indeed, my sins are mine
and all my miss-deeds stand in line
so never mind a god that forgives them.
When the test of time reveals me
I will wear them.

I haven't found a name for grace
or found salvation in a book or face
although I've read the bibles of so many
so I try to ply my days with deeds of light
and perform good acts for goodness sake.

I found my light in distant stars, in skies
that rain to cleanse our deepest scars,
and swore to fight the violent blight,
to mend the plight of Venus
with the healing of mars
and raise my brightest songs to flight,
to sing my gentle words to night...

that someone hear them from behind the bars
of the charlatans that fool ya,
that someone raise their eyes up high
to see this deepest word alight
in minds that open to rebirth

at the sight of a broken   hallelujah

Ill Winds

blow with leper-breath and fire.
Epithets form on kiss lips at
the holocaust footage on screens
that Norman Rockwell used to paint
with children at play in Mayberry

but tea-baggers and corporate ravens
killed Opie and Goober -
poisoned the fishin' hole
as the national anthem
was played on the drums
of cannibals

Ill winds chase white bears out to sea
while we, those next extinct dragons
breathe fire

Frost

(for Samuel Taylor Coleridge)

 I woke to spy a million gems
as if god's breath had frozen fast
and every bough the cold condemns
was varnished by her icy blast.

I wondered what poems she spoke
to decorate the forest so,
to paint each tree with brilliant cloak,
to make the day awake with glow.

I hear her sing through emerald pines
and taste her touch in watercress
that grows where winter's streams recline,
and by these precious greens am blessed.

The sun awoke these earthbound stars
as if to salve my soul's bleak scars.

Howling at Giants

I'm writing because I don't have the breath to scream –
because we're selling our children's dreams.
The giants do not court my beautiful brain, don't
caress me with care or soothe my pain,
don't revere the drop of moon's fragile egg
or refrain from marching like green weapons
to red fields beneath flags of profit,
and conglomerates coagulate like a tide
that never quickens with life.
Profane, these prophets of bloody gain; PROFANE!

I'm writing because my voice cracks like distant small arms fire
that raises the ire of any mother at the copper scent of war,
HOWLING at the sycophants - that choir that sings for the embryo
but aborts the poor in war at age twenty-one; aborts the poor
with another word for god, aborts the very heart of man;
SCREAMING to the most holy grandmother in all of us
to rewire our leaders by force of upraised voice.

My strident pen rankles at the sight of this.
A kiss, a deep moist kiss used to bring such bliss,
and sex exist to put such earthly ambition aside,
but the giants persist in painting landscapes with so many corpses
that any celebration of life seems remiss in addressing
the bodies piled in banks, and a lover's eyes
can not dismiss such holocaust as this.

Since my lover's arms are weak, and voice is thin,
I'll howl into the electronic universe, plead with the last open minds,
HOWL my chagrin to heavens devoid of hope to begin the
revolution, to remind the giants that they are made up of us,
from the CEO of Exxon to my wee grandbaby, Finn.

We ended a war in seventy-five, and by all good intentions still alive,
WE CAN DO IT AGAIN!

Will you join me? Just pick up your pen

The Far Edge of Autumn

The man is dry, as if his leaves
depart; his pages lean toward a picture
on the back of his spine. His castanet heart
wears a wife-beater to run, run, run
between mobile homes and libraries;
a fun-boy chasing toys and
female genitals across decades and thorns.

Pry as he might at sty or silken thigh, he still
sups alone, still fashions nooses of words
to tie in his spilling intestines, bereft
of any scheme or secret map, scribbled
on a bar-napkin or a cardinal's fat breast.

He nears a nest... perhaps some sylvan shore
where frolic wears a thong and a maiden-face;
perhaps a firing squad, populated by his sheep,
gutted in fits of self-importance and erection.
He will not recline erect on some cross, or
scribble himself across a granite face,
but ghost himself into the leaves of time;
wasting eternity in the stacks,
his ribs aligned like sonnets.

Blue Heron

Stalking the shallows in clown shoes,
peering past your trusty saber,
you seek providence in wet clues -
a plump amphibian neighbor.

You, like a statue of a limb,
adorn the shore of lake or stream,
awaiting the approach of brim,
(that tiny fish the books call bream.)

Your voice, it seems is always hoarse
but, elegant in your bearing
and wielding sword with awful force,
you raise high the fish you're snaring.

This gorgeous bird with ugly voice
is not a predator by choice.

Apple

I watched an apple from
blossom to fall   to the
stomach of a raccoon
and understood
holy shit.

Dead Air

I tried to write a radio poem
with a silent pen
again, and yet again, no children
were born of limp instrument
I was in the elephant's graveyard
of verse, the desert
A reeking corpse left no tracks
on parchment, consumed
by raven's beak
Even the bleakest of vistas hid
still born fetuses, crumpled
around my feet like fallen planets
and rumpled heroes left
bar-napkins, naked and unadorned
left the monsters to their grim folly
left the right to scream NO
into my children's dim future
left a lover's breast cold
untouched by the caress of verse
or the memory of the widower
that looked out over the gun-sight
to find the light of words
to guide him home from night
only to find me quiet, uncaring
It is not moot to ponder death
at the sound of dead air
not moot to question breath
when one has forgotten
how to sing

Lost

(for Ted Hughes and dear Sylvia)

Two poets were lost in a feather bed
lost to quickening verb
and repast of full moon's
dearest nouns

Sculpted of warmest clay, she lay
supine, flushed by the light
of his fingers

and by his sight, he found her
by his touch, his scent, and
by the very taste of her
was he transformed

a poet, and full-formed as lover
As spelunker of holy cave
as chronicler of sighs
he shuddered

What shapes she formed
of transcendental arch
what verse of cries
she uttered in guttural groan
like a cello in a secret key

But on this feathered plain of love
who was the rider, who the steed?

First her, and later – he
as truly love was meant to be
in my imagination

because poet superior
is the position for me

Black Cat in the Rain

She did me like Maybelline, and the sky
fell like rain –
city rain, cold rain that cleans nothin'.

My Mojo hand was rollin' snake-eyes
and everbody on State Street knew me,
knew me by my shotgun breath, my steam,
knew that straight-razor smile meant
hurtin' time was wearin' my watch
out for a spin in the rain –

but somehow, that rain was holy - holy
like an ol' hollow-body Gibson
with no fret board, like a cuckold's heart
or a sharecropper's billfold, cold, hard,
like the sound of the string that broke
when I smelled him on her.

I left my Black Lightnin' at home
'cause I needed my voice fer drinkin'
an' I needed to hear a bluesman holler
'cause nobody can sing that wet blue night

like a black cat in the rain.

Whistle-stop

 Brakes clenched, sparks lit the night
The box-car echoed with questions

I grew in her belly like cancer
but Kerouac called from Mexico –
louder than factories, mortgages
or shame

At the crossroads, I wrote a poem
about a bastard

Hangin' with the Dead

They came to me like autumn's fire
   & gnash winter's teeth
   through long blue nights
They seem to scent proximity, as I
   blink opener eyes at war
   & learn in the light of time
   how wee am I , but bright
   in ember's dying flame

As mosquito merchants drain my purse
   the funerals curse my days
   & the chorus of night
   gains voices
but the sweat and heat breed poems
   as if these ghosts have psalms
   to sing through the pen
   of a confidante

These, then, are the winter poems
   that moan like specter's verse
   as an inferno approaches ash
   to remind my fellows
   that the reign of light is short
   and every day, a dance

A Ladder to the Moon

I built a ladder to the moon.
It wound in circles, like
the secrets left written
by a pebble's kiss of pond
or a breast.
 I tried to build one to Venus -
tried to build it with words,
but even the beats knew not
the way to Venus.

She loved me anyway
and I only needed the one.

Death of a Lover

When two souls and two bodies meld as one,
and cycles of seasons cement that troth,
it seems our mate is vibrant as the sun.
Each step along life's path is shared by both.

When two have shared love's most magical quest,
and combined to multiply by dint of moon
as if their giddy rhythm has been blessed,
this is love from which poetry is hewn.

We complete a circle like Yin and Yang
when we surrender to such love as this
and distance gnaws at us like hunger pangs.
Blessed is the couple that knows such bliss.

How then, may a lover like me atone
for the guilt of leaving her all alone?

Bleed

 A Poet must commit truth
in a time of falsehood
be a seer in the kingdom
of the blind

He must write from the
uterus
and she from her nads

She must not shriek "ICE"
in a burning room
or he conspire in war

We must of all
bleed words

On the Cusp

The trees have shed their gaudy cloaks
to bare the ground to season's chill.
The only leaves aloft are oak;
one last painting atop the hill.

We see deer as venison now,
in the gloaming of the season.
Its time to mount that heavy plow
against depths of winter's treason.

Prior to blue, we freeze in gray
as cold November rains cast a pall.
In front of stoves, the children play,
outside, orange men shoot holes in fall.

Stick season, it seems, has arrived,
and the skeletons have revived.

They sway atop gnarly spires
as if to grasp at stormy skies
or reach aloft for sun's fire.
The wind strums their song with a sigh.

These sentinels, braced against North,
gird us against the icy wind
as first flakes of snow sally forth
as if hungry for those who've sinned.

Their blood recedes beneath cold ground
as if to dodge the icy grip
of wind that seethes in brittle crowns.
Ice marches south, but they're equipped.

This cusp of time, between the two
makes seasons merge, and poets blue.

Poor Boys

Oh, those poor boys.
They hear the alarms on the farms, in the ghettos
and jump into Uncle Sam's bloody arms.
They paint themselves in patriotic uniforms
say goodbye to Betty-Sue and put themselves
into harm's way for lucre and tradition, for greedy
old men who skipped THEIR turns to burn
with red, white, and blue fervor, to burn with
napalm and crispy critters, to die for their daddies
pride.

Oh, those poor boys and girls.
Old merchants bought politicians with dirty dollars,
hollered at those boys and girls about duty,
about glory and money, education and riches,
if they live, freedom won with poor blood
flooding rich coffers, flag-draped coffins
and more fucking guns if they lose the bet,
twenty one shots from seven barrels, making
them all cringe like grandpa when he hears
a helicopter, cringe like
mothers.

Oh, those greedy old fucks!
that prey on the corpse of the middle-class,
prey on the ones that are down on their luck,
the ones that ain't got the big bucks for college,
the ones with a lot of courage, that pluck them
from good families and return them FUBAR –
FUCKED UP BEYOND ALL RECOGNITION.
Those greedy old men that can't hear god sing,
can't hear freedom ringing in the ears
of nations that don't conform to the norm
of subservience to the red white and blue
machine, those green and gray monsters,
those men that cling to property, those colonial
bullies.

Oh, the fathers and mothers
That send progeny to feed the beast, that
offer their young to the cannibalistic cabal
that advertizes for folks with the least
to offer up sacred sacrifice of sons and daughters
to pose as corpses in the ledgers of endless
ones and zeros, for riches gained by the pain
of their get, that bet the lives of heroes
to move lines on maps, lines on faces
of grieving mothers, others that sell poppies
on holidays, never mind the fields of
Afghanistan; never mind the races that are
inordinately numerous at Arlington;
never mind the kind of boys they choose;
never mind the ones they never lose,
safe in the arms of America, that its on poor
bones that the monster chews.

Oh, man

now, we have TWO wars going!
Look at all the seeds of war we're sewing!
These ones over here want you to die for god,
while that one over yonder had an odd god,
so he's gotta go, sure as snow in December!
Remember the sixties, "give peace a chance?"
Remember how we used to dance while we
chanted, singing, "All we are aaaasking"
while they beat us, those brainwashed sons
of the great unwashed while the sons of the
senators basked in the arms of Betty-Lou?

Well, now, its our boat, an' we're rowing,
an' the seeds of war we're sewing are sprouting
in our children. We're bloodying the sand
to keep the oil flowing, to keep a face-shooter's
stock in Halliburton high, sending our babies
to die, killing some brown mama's babies
'cause they have oil, odd gods, and folks that
kill us for killing them, and the fucking wheel
keeps turning and Rome, it seems, is always

burning.

Release

I kept you in my pen for years -
   squirming, writhing, making
   my palm sweat.
I let you out a trickle at a
   time when I held you like a
   glass slipper in a torrent
or a time when you were honey
   in the wintergreen - symphony.
I let you out to scream like god
   as you split like amoeba
   to bear Venus to my arms.
I let you out to paint
   you in the river, to frame it
   in yellow, to stroke you with
   words for water over stone.

Now I release you to lean close

to hear my last poem.

While Children Burn

 can you warm yourself
by the fire beneath my scalp -
find calm in these stanzas -
these vespers of peace
that whisper childlike pleas
for love?

Nope

Planting Time

I plant corn to hold the sky up,
spinach to gird me against tomorrow.
I planted the children like flowers
reflected in the lake of your smile.
I have fed this soil, and will.
I sift it through reverent fingers
like decades or blood, taste it
like sorrow and jubilation.
It smells like a lifetime of dusty poems.
Sometimes my rows form circles.
Plant me beneath the asters that bloom
beyond the reach of time, and remember
our germination.

Bombing The Moon

Another poet is dying
and we're bombing the moon.

The seasons are confused
and the aged consume
the young.

Metapixels and anthems
blare from entrancer screens
where foxes fleece lemmings.

 Oh Venus! that lost us to Mars
Oh cannibal-virus-man
with such science as this,
what have we wrought
of ego's steel but doom?

 Oh Mamma! vast blue womb,
what rape do we provide
by inventing gods
to forgive us this?

Another poet is dying
and we're bombing the moon.

Heavy Horses

It starts with that red bloom,
that holy volcano, sucked into
the syringe to mix with that
dependable suicide.

Breastmilk, doom, lover, assassin,
gift of flower, motherfucker, light of
the east, finally, beast;

You rode over me like a herd
of heavy horses.

I love you.

Poem Farm

From my front porch, I
see poems everywhere.
Where the forest meets the
prairie, and beyond to the
mother of waters, characters
abound, in the clouds, even
beneath the old plow.

They grow in the garden
like zucchinis we leave on
porches - and run,
like multitudes of tomatoes
that seldom ripen.

Poems sing in the night
with coyote voices, with
chapped lips in the long
blue chill of crackling
winter.

They whisper colors from
the first daffodil to the
chattering of last rusted leaf.

The plow truck has stories
to tell, the scythe, the bones
in the sheep-shed, the
vociferous raven, the toad
with the Buddha spirit.

I write back in time, to the
veined hand on the plowshare,
the ringing of the dinner-bell;
I hear the silent voices singing
ancient lullabies to babies
in a drawer. I write of
Whitman's ghosts.

My pen is disenchanted
with now, but old smiles
grow new stanzas
on a farm that
hides me in
the past.

The Quiet Machine

"C'mon, start!" I holler

Kick, cajole, swear
One asthmatic wheeze
and all is silent, blank

I check the plugs, the coil
the carb where it mixes
the filter I bypass anyway
the fuel

"Fuel, that's it!
Here, steal a metaphor
that's the ticket!
Daffodil!"

Nothing, not a stanza
not a line, nada, bupkis
blank paper

I have to write a poem
and I sit like a limp porn star
like an honest politician
nothing to say

What did Kerouac do
when he was blocked?
"Ahh, a Haiku..."

the bud never bloomed
scents of silence fill August
virgin flowers die

Of Wolves and Dogs

A poem attacked me today
at the bait shop like heroin
or a woman I abused myself with,
stabbing me again in my sleep.

Lines stalk me at rare leisure.

"Now, the wolves are eating our dogs!"
he said, unhappy with the dept.
of unnatural resources.

The machine started of its own accord
like it does when confronted by
lightning, love, republicans, a breast.

Perhaps the wolves are the poetry
and I, a consumed dog, (god, after -
all spelled backwards.)

The wolf-machine consumes idle
moments with empathy or doom,
with lines that bloom like those
unlikely flowers atop thistle.

I need to howl at warlords, at
clergy and commerce, howl
as a fresh stanza bleeds, enslaved
by this need to draw attention
to the latest inconsequential death.

Perhaps that is why my poems
end with a song
and a snarl.

Wearing God Out

The rain is my cloak, the moon, my shield,
and I stand behind my rhymes like oak.
I whisper love songs over the killing fields,
love songs sewn without thimbles
in the spastic throes of such love as stars
that part the gracious lips of night,
that part the bars of trepidation's jail
to light the way to the dipper's pail;
the way to the plains where friction
plants sighs, aural flowers; ghosts
where lovers plied soft flesh.

My god is rounder than Buddha's belly
and her psalms, the voices on each breeze.
I pound my prayers on plastic keys
as if to shout into the void that gods are
not found in mirrors, but in the very soil.
We toil for oil like lemmings leaping
or ants at work constructing a vast
magnifying glass with which to amass
a fortune formed of ash.

I wear my faith on dirty hands,
beneath my nails, on denim.
I go to church in a garden
and sing with the rain.

Now the rain is acid
and I only write
of pain.

Watercress

I have a secret emerald
where winter's mysteries sharpen
like nipples to December stars

whispers from lips of brook
guide me to her immortal garden

a fissure in the grounded clouds
a glistening of moving moist
and the first taste

blooms with a quiver

Warlord at the Diner

I saw a metaphor in the ditch -
white head painted by gore
from a bloated deer
or a friend; perhaps a
patriot.

The ooze covering his plumage
was organic ochre
as if this de-evolutionary
was already halfway
home

High Coup

There it was dancing
like a star on a string
like a nearly ripe apple

the metaphor

nipples hard voice primed
to spin some rhyme to
illuminate some conspicuous

noun

can't reach metaphor
must imbibe

there
a nude ballerina dancing
after a distant star
or a lightning bug blinking
down the prairie path

to the crick
"the path less traveled"
must be the way to Sam's

Xanadu

 didn't reach the star
but I caught the lightning

bug

"As the elders of our time choose to remain blind
let us rejoice, let us sing and dance"

Donovan Phillips Leitch

Bliss - Bombs

While the potentates recreate
with currency, with carnage, with
power that grows by the hour -

we of the poet's tribe, the artists,
dance.

While our mother weeps acid tears
and all our fears limp home to roost
it is not moot to sing -

to take new shapes in ill winds,
to bend fearful lips
to a kiss.

It is this that may still the warlords -
a song, a dance, a poem -
a kiss,

bliss...

Another one for Walt

Oh resident, citizen of the Mississippi river drainage,
    denizen of fertile field, raise tired eyes
    to the sky that author's rain, proclaim wet miracle.

Oh dreamer, whose mind's eye wanders as water
    meanders to distant estuary, where mystery lies
    betwixt those fertile bottoms, and the ocean
    beckons to the sailor with hidden vistas in mind.

The river tugs at heartstrings like a catfish
    at an earthworm gob, stalwart farmer, pulling
    at a corn-cob pipe, a farm-boy, clumsy
    in attempts to breach Mary-Lou's bra-strap –

    like the salty gulf that beckons her south.

Oh corn, that rustles in the Midwest night,
    a gold more actual than that which resides in the
    purse of the merchant or the cleric, stretch
    in your might across the very land
    where the Sioux and the Iroquois thrived
    before the muskets brought the sins of dollars
    and that blaring cacophony of plans.

Soooooooooie! brings home the hogs, whooooooooie!
    rings the refrain of children at play in the big muddy
    until the clang of a well-worn bell sings dinner songs.
    It is Sunday, and the stingy chicken waits.

Oh, Mary-Lou, in your gingham and yeast, sing
    your lullaby to cherub's soft cheek, it is this meek
    child that will next till the fields of god, that will
    wear the very earth beneath his nails, carry pails
    of warm milk to new generations of robust
    farmers that know that every furrow leads them home.

It is significant that the softest teat draws the callused hand,
    draws the nation of man to suckle at the tip of the
    big rock candy mountain, to seek the mother heat
    of purest heart and feed the daughters of the world.

Oh, yondering boy, put feet to new paths, and till new land,
    with a weather eye for angry skies, hold dear ones near
    and treasure idle times to your heart's delight,
    but keep the river in sight.

Oh, the fisherman, beneath the mighty oak, thrive in moments
    that defy the wealthy gent, soothe your spirit
    beside the current that renders gravity holy,
    that you repent ambition in times of bliss, kiss the river
    with the innocent toes of your long lost boy,
    young again in idle worship of timeless tides,

    to know that despite man's folly,
    the river abides,

    and hear the water

                                sing.

The Storm of 2010

The wind shrieks like a catamount in furious embrace.
Battalions of snowflakes march in horizontal fury.
The fallen limbs, entwined, decorate the roads like lace.
Tempest-tossed, we struggle, enmeshed in a frigid flurry.
 Anonymous, we hide. The lines are down, we're off the grid!
Beneath our quilts, we mimic the jubilant cries of wind,
in search of the joy and comfort the ghastly gale forbids,
while outside, the angry zephyr gyrates in whirls and spins.
 Metaphoric politicians hurl invectives like sleet
as conservative candidates attempt to storm the gates,
fueled by ignorant sheep that bleat at puppet master's feet.
The meek just huddle, afraid, hoping the storm will abate.
 This autumn turbulence is a fearful thing to behold,
as I see the visage of America turning cold.

Saturday Night in Bohemia

Spittle on the microphone
and the thighs
of the nondescript, stewed blond,
with the skewed thong -
funky, spunky, desperate, another
midnight madonna, quickly forgotten

amidst the roaches and piss,
burnin' one with the boys
behind the dumpster,
behind the open mic bar,
behind twenty-three lines
and half a bottle of Makers,
and still I read, still
hearing Alex' sax, still
tasting desperate sex,
reading for the rats, the alley cats,
the swooping bats, in all their
diseased membranes
and grimy finery, still giving the moon
an excuse to cast aspersions
on the character of mirth,
reading for the very girth of night
in fair Bohemia

on a perfect Saturday night.

Chequamegon Sunrise

Another Saturday Night has become
another Sunday mourning
I should be going to church
or writing a Haiku
but I don't know God or
Japanese

I think I peed on the stone
Buddha again last night
and my mouth tastes
like ass

but I just watered the garden
and remembered the coyotes
singing with my flute
at midnight

The hummingbirds are awake
and sunrise was everyday
magic

Reading Ginsy

saved me from the likes of Billy C
'cause see, pabulum just don't
appeal to me.
Billy dumbed it down, made poetry plain,
made academic drones write
to entertain, with dry little jokes
and dry little words
like Dick and fucking Jane,
wrote poems about nothing much
for dry little men in the domain
of cubicles, a boring refrain of rivers he never fished,
calluses he never raised, never profane,
never controversial, no new language
he'd have to explain, just buffoonery in
a plain brown wrapper, poetry that never strains
the tiny mind, but with a wry joke
that's supposed to make you feel clever
for getting it, mainstreet in fucking Mayberry
or Lake Woebegone, a veritable symphony
of the mundane, the bain of my brain,
cluttering public radio waves
and bland journals, cocaine for the dim.
I bet that puerile motherfucker even
voted for Mc cain.

Allen was a horse of another color
like Zelda Fitzgerald or good old Walt,
like ordering escargot with a chocolate malt.
Yeah, I had to take his references
to big sweaty balls with a dose of salt,
but he knocked my brain
right out of the box. My own poetry is all
Allen's fault, treasure from my mind's odd vault.

Howl was an assault on the senses,
unlocking the arcade of words to
paint pictures we'd never seen,
preening on the page like gaudy birds,
no abcs or one-two-threes,

no Hallmark crap or predictable pap for the masses,
not the sing-song rhyme from poetry classes,
but words to provoke minds to awaken,
to rip the rose colored glasses from the upturned nose
of the academic beast and assault the senses
of the eager masses and bring a halt
to boredom in poetry, to poetry in boxes,
to exalt in the different and spice the bland
diet of the collective mind of a nation
on the brink of a psychedelic revolution,
to make us dance to the tune of poetry's evolution.

Thanks to Allen Ginsberg, I write the spoken word,
the smokin' word, the words that herds
of misbegotten politicians don't want heard,
words to incite the herds of sheep to question
authority, words to ignite the imagination,
to overexcite the neurons of the collective consciousness,
to invite the tea-party to understand the plight
of the non-white, non-hetero, non-Christian,
hordes of we're America too, god dammit!

Thanks to Allen, the beat rises again like
that hippy from the middle-east, rises like
a new drumbeat with an age-old refrain, rises like
smoke signals over a battlefield where the poor
bleed for the wealthy, a healthy voice in a poisonous
wind, a phoenix from the ashes of the American dream,
a keening voice that stalks midnight microphones
from Rockland to Wounded knee, from coast to coast,
from sea to shining sea, that preaches freedom
in the land of the free, and bravery to write loud again
in the home of the fucking brave, to brave the torrent
of academic bullshit about nothing much
and fill a river of words with the beat
of rainbow drummers and the audacity
to preach peace in the face of warriors,
to exercise the full measure of the first amendment
in the nation of religious wars and corporate whores,
rivers of words and ideas, rivers full of justice and equality,
rivers of hope in a world gone mad.

Thank you Mr. Ginsberg…

Thistles and Moonbeams

Oh, I could over-compensate like Hemingway
could have married a dumb girl with a great
head of blond hair and propped up breasts
but I had to put myself to the test

I like a nice set of brains on my women
like to bleed my way to that sweet flower
like a woman with the power of her convictions
and the ability to stomach mine

I like to see her naked when the moon watches
the fireflies write their metaphor for shooting
stars, like to show off my scars from her sharp
tongue, her wreath of thorns, her rebukes

I like to see her naked in the garden, wrangling
cucumber vines or pulling weeds, or at the lake
on an august night, like the way she plays
the bullshit card when I pontificate

Sure, I need to suture the wounds from her sharp
tongue, plug the tears in my ego with emotional
duct-tape, but I wouldn't have it any other way
The top of the thistle is where the moonbeams

go to play

My last poem

will be whispered, as my very words fail
to spring from leaky bellows, and the Marlboro man
has his say
and all the fallen poets wait for their newest fellow
The poem, I think, will be yellow, the color of sun
and round, somehow, like the passage of the moon
It will be no dirge, but a hopeful tune
from a jejune spirit, a lilting child, at play in the fields
of forever
That poem will not be punctuated, as infinity need
no barriers, no walls or breadcrumbs for the timid mind
but only some gracious noun that resembles everything

The poem will have breasts, as I can attest to love
for lovely glands and the crinkled proof of love's finesse
and the spring from which every poet crawled
to scrawl the face of love across such graceful pages
that every reader swoon at the beauty of her smile
miles and stanzas of text that so enrich the heart of man
that songs are made of these, and lullabies to soothe
a babe to sleep, and keep sorrow at bay

With breath near gone, but eyes alight perceiving grace
the pace of it will be slow, reverent in the naming
of beauty, the softest vocalization of granite love
and the liquid flow of river's tide, following moon to sea
and the soul of a poet, finding another way to be

In life's lee, at death's door, such happiness will reverberate
that springs of tears dry before they exit eyes that
know I know that what's in store is so lovely
that adjectives for beauty spill like rain
and pain is left at the doorway to Xanadu

The demons that populate my earlier works
will cower in sunlit nooks, exposed to the gracious
light that caps the world, that lets love's flag unfurl
over lands that need no fences or maps
but only drums to circle tribes in one true dance

Oh, the romance of that last poem
The only one that really matters, leaving the
matters of warrior and commerce to the corporeal
to splay across the very sky like proverbs
in the breath of the world
left behind

on graduation day

Still Life with Barbed Wire

I saw a storm of horses

blow across the prairie

like clear waters

running to the sea

or simple words seeking

apt companions like

body and electric

and I knew that

sometimes, god is

a broken fence.

Birthday Poem 2011

How will I spend my last birthday?

Will I forsake the post-nasal-drip
of the gun-metal sky
to write of daffodils or the way
a nipple crinkles under the
ministrations of love?

The future seethes
with maggots and republicans,
and my breathing remembers
every smokestack, every
Marlboro moment, every
nigger joke, every gay joke,
every dead aboriginal, every
wounded river, oozing a
sepia path South into
my grand-daughter's
future, every war, and another moron
from Texas pontificates
on the news.

They lit my candles in Minnesota
a week ago and the phlegm
is writing odd German
syllables.

The view from here is bleak,
and the sun too tired to paint
my day.

I want to dance with Dorothy,
but the yellowbrickroad
was paved over last year
to provide parking for the new
superwalmart.

I want to eat lobster,
but they are babies from
a ruined sea, want a steak, but
well, Cargill, want exuberant sex,
but the twentyfourhournewscycle ate
my laughter, my erection, and I reflect on
the coming election, the horror of the choices,
the greed that feeds them all from the same corporate
chalise.

Perhaps, a funeral for the corn, a resurrection
for the wilting cabbage, a sweet carrot, pried
from the ground that will shelter me, that last
stubborn pea, clinging to the vine…like me.

Maybe I'll brave the rain, the pain,
whistle greensleeves one more time
in the autumnal rot, or roll around
in Baudelair's dark flowers, dance
with Anne's furies, sing happy songs
in the occasional flurries, or put on that
happy mask, so faded and cracked.

I look down on Mother Superior's face,
and even the Apostles seem to mock me.

Happy freakin' birthday.

Return of the Toad With the Buddha Spirit

Was it his texture, his solidarity with the soil,
or his gaze?
The calm in those dark orbs,
the very Yoda, Yogi, the Tai Chi
of the way he stretched each leg,
his disregard of me as if
he knew the foundation, the garden
were really his. These beautied warts.

After the daffodils, after the bold iris,
he oozed out to take his place
beside the rose's gnarled feet,
and he silently whispered
the secrets of circles.

When a flesh toad lives
between a stone Buddha and a rose,
something blooms like
rain.

The Weight of Worlds

I behold the weight of worlds in anguished eyes,
   in the cries of the farmers at the hail,
   the cancered man, looking too deep.
No exit, the young man bawls at yondering love,
   but I can not catch him as he falls,
   or still the screams of the poor soldier.
I grieve with the mother of the hungry child, the
   wild-eyed loner, beneath some dark eclipse,
   gnash my teeth at wild and unfair fate,
   but I can't recreate glee for sorrow's mate.

Oh, the weight of worlds I hear in garbled moans;
   what remedy or solace may I provide
   to a survivor, or that wounded cuckold?
What groans may poems turn to song, or bright verse
   alleviate when the very sun goes dark?
How may I sleep through dried and brittle crops,
   or with the resound of distant screams,
   when I have seen the chaos of soldier's dreams?
Abed, I thrash with the agony of my troubled species,
   as if each flower painted by careful words
   withers in all the weeping I have heard.

The weight of worlds has attached itself to me
   and Shakespeare's question occurs
   as my clock strikes a metaphysical
   twenty-three,   "to be or not to be?"

Salmon Fishing on the Sioux

Déjà vu again, this lurching
in my throat,
the moisture,

the panties on my radio antennae.

I went fishing: I remember that,
salmon,
chasing the rain back

up the river...

The End

www.ingramcontent.com/pod-product-compliance
Lightning Source LLC
Chambersburg PA
CBHW032038080426
42733CB00006B/117